Poverty and In
Early Years Eauᴄᴀᴛ.

CW01064509

Poverty and Inclusion in Early Years Education will help practitioners to understand the experiences of young children who are living in poverty. It examines the potentially devastating impact of poverty and social exclusion on children's chances in later life, and considers recent policy and practice reforms which have recognised the critical role played by Early Years settings and practitioners in guaranteeing a secure foundation for children's future attainment.

The book explores the historical, political and legal aspects of policy on poverty and social exclusion, before offering guidance on how practitioners can help to address the inequalities caused by poverty and break the cycle of deprivation. Chapters go on to address the practicalities of working with children, families and agencies to create an inclusive Early Years environment, and focus on issues including:

- developing effective partnerships with families;
- collaborating with outside agencies;
- encouraging awareness of different socio-economic backgrounds.

With case studies, reflective questions and further reading included throughout to help the reader to apply the ideas to their own practice, the book will be an invaluable resource for Early Years practitioners, students and all those wishing to promote social inclusion and tackle the impact of social exclusion and poverty in Early Years settings.

Mark Cronin is Senior Lecturer in Early Childhood Education and Care, Newman University, UK. He has worked in both the Local Authority and voluntary sector as a children and families social worker. Mark's interests include safeguarding, social policy and working with children and families.

Karen Argent is former Senior Lecturer in Early Childhood Education and Care at Newman University, UK. She worked as an inclusion worker on one of the first Sure Start programmes and is a co-founder of the Letterpress Project. Her research interests include representations of diversity in children's literature.

Chris Collett is former Senior Lecturer in Early Childhood Education and Care at Newman University, UK, where she specialised in SEND and inclusion. Chris has taught children and young people with moderate to profound learning disabilities for 25 years and was a Local Authority advisory teacher for children under 5 with SEND.

Diversity and Inclusion in the Early Years

Disability and Inclusion in Early Years Education
Chris Collett

Gender Diversity and Inclusion in Early Years Education
Kath Tayler and Deborah Price

LGBT Diversity and Inclusion in Early Years Education
Deborah Price and Kath Tayler

Poverty and Inclusion in Early Years Education
Mark Cronin, Karen Argent and Chris Collett

Series page: https://www.routledge.com/education/series/EARLYYEARS

Poverty and Inclusion in Early Years Education

Mark Cronin, Karen Argent and Chris Collett

LONDON AND NEW YORK

First published 2017
by Routledge
2 Park Square, Milton Park, Abingdon, Oxon OX14 4RN

and by Routledge
711 Third Avenue, New York, NY 10017

Routledge is an imprint of the Taylor & Francis Group, an informa business

British Library Cataloguing-in-Publication Data
A catalogue record for this book is available from the British Library

Library of Congress Cataloging-in-Publication Data
A catalog record for this book has been requested

ISBN: 9781138201491 (hbk)
ISBN: 9781138201507 (pbk)
ISBN: 9781315511696 (ebk)

Typeset in Optima
by Deanta Global Publishing Services, Chennai, India
Printed and bound by CPI Group (UK) Ltd, Croydon, CR0 4YY

To Lily, Archie, Naomi, Boden and all children everywhere

Contents

Contents

Illustrations

Figures

Boxes

Foreword

Since this book was written, the UK has watched unfold the terrible events of 14 June 2017, when fire ripped through the Grenfell Tower housing block causing terrible loss of life and devastating consequences for many, many more.

What seems to be emerging in the aftermath of the tragedy stands as a powerful illustration of the key themes discussed throughout this book; the powerlessness and lack of voice experienced by the residents, both leading up to and after the fire, and the clear contempt with which residents were and are treated, by both local and national government officials, purely on the grounds that they are poor. It has become apparent too that this is a pattern replicated across Local Authorities in England.

It would be reassuring to think that the horror of Grenfell Tower could be a catalyst for real change, but already there are strong indications that the focus of any investigations will be on the detail – faulty cladding – and not the broader, and more damaging, social housing policy. The increasing privatisation of housing services (provision and maintenance), has effectively removed the accountability, and therefore culpability from local and national government, leaving responsibility for social housing in the hands of those whose primary aim is to make a profit.

The likely outcome is that a few councillors will resign, and perhaps some company executives will be prosecuted – some may even be convicted in the criminal courts. Certainly, building regulations will be 'tightened'. But at the end of it all, housing policy for the most vulnerable in our society will remain the same – a low priority provided at a minimum cost, because the message is, as always, that the poor don't matter.

All the more important then, that those working in the early years with children and families understand this deeply prejudicial approach, not just to housing but to all social policy, for what it is, and make it their duty to question and challenge these current and ongoing strategies that affect the poorest in their settings and communities.

We hope that this book will equip you, whether student or practitioner, to do just that.

Introduction

Mark Cronin

The Early Years Education context has clearly been identified by recent governments as one of the preferred locations for addressing social inequalities. The extension of the free provision of early learning places for vulnerable 2-year-old children is clear evidence of an ongoing intention to position Early Years settings and practitioners at the forefront of attempts to maximise children's potential, by providing a secure foundation for their future attainment and life chances. There are a number of external factors that can thwart that potential, including those relating to disability, gender and ethnicity, and since the end of the twentieth century the role of poverty has been highlighted. This book aims to provide a comprehensive but straightforward guide to the inclusion of children who are living in poverty that offers a clear policy context, exploring the rationale for this focus on Early Years settings, and also a comprehensive resource to support good practice.

Since the introduction of the Child Poverty Act 2010 and the requirement for the government to annually report on the prevalence of child poverty in the UK and the commitments made to reduce child poverty in respect of specific 2020 targets, social policy reforms have attempted to identify strategies for realising these goals. Subsequent government reviews, such as the Allen Review 'Early Intervention: The Next Steps' (Allen 2011), clearly locate interventions with children in the 0–3 age range as pivotal to breaking the cycle of deprivation, and the Tickell Review (2011) acknowledges the key role to be played by the Early Years Foundation Stage curriculum in providing the essential foundations for their achievement through school. The rapid expansion of the free provision of early learning places for children from 2 to 4 years old is a key feature of the government's attempts to reduce child poverty, both in terms of providing childcare for working parents and providing a foundation for children's educational achievement. Alongside these developments, we have seen the proliferation of powerful negative media discourses in respect of the representation of poverty and social exclusion that need to be understood and critically challenged if practitioners are going to be prepared to work with children and families in these circumstances. This book, therefore, explores the context for these social policy reforms and strategies employed in Early Years settings which aim to reduce child poverty.

The book will begin by setting the policy context for poverty and inclusion in the Early Years, reminding readers of its historical origins in respect of children's rights (UNCRC) and a focus on 'Educare' reforms, which located Early Years Education at the centre of attempts to tackle social exclusion and the effects of child poverty. The United Nations Convention on the Rights of the Child (UNCRC) (UNICEF 1989) was and is the most comprehensive statement of children's rights ever produced and is the most widely ratified international human rights treaty in history. Therefore, it is an important benchmark against which we can review our progress towards meeting the needs of children and protecting their rights. This book will go on to look at both the current policy and practice reforms which guide Early Years providers, as well as examining and challenging the associated dominant discourses which inform practice. It will explain what can be done to create an inclusive Early Years environment that supports children and their families, in terms of tackling the impact of social exclusion and poverty. The book will also explore good practice in working with families and outside agencies in order to create an inclusive environment where children can reach their potential.

There are key themes throughout the book which underpin its approach to exploring the lives of children and families experiencing poverty and social exclusion and the nature of practitioner interventions:

- Commonly held beliefs about the experience of poverty are increasingly affected by dominant discourses (media and policy), which identify poverty as a consequence of individual failure and which do not take adequate account of broader structural factors which impact on children and families.

- The Early Years has been the subject of significant social policy focus, which has located practitioners in this sector at the frontline of early interventions in terms of tackling poverty and social exclusion.

- There is a need to support Early Years practitioners to understand the values/ideas which are currently driving social policy approaches to working with children and families who experience poverty and social exclusion. Integral to this process is the need to engage in some critical self-evaluation, which aims to empower them to exercise their own professional judgements in respect of what represents good practice in this context.

- Early Years practitioners are ideally placed to support children and families who are experiencing poverty and social exclusion and have the capacity to develop models of good practice.

The book has been organised into two distinct sections, the first of which is entitled 'Understanding the Issues' (Chapters 2, 3 and 4) and is designed to provide a clear context for working with children and families, both in terms of providing an understanding of the impact of poverty and social exclusion on children and families, and the legal and policy environment in which this work takes place. These first four chapters will also explore different explanations of the relationship between poverty and outcomes, for example, do people experience poverty as a consequence of making poor lifestyle choices, or does inherent inequality in society disadvantage some people? It will also explore to what degree these different explanations have been influential in defining the ways in which we are encouraged to work with the children and families experiencing poverty and social exclusion. A chapter will explore the impact of relative access to social and cultural capital in respect of social mobility and overall it intends to broaden the discussion to enable a comprehensive understanding of the dynamics involved in the experience of poverty and social exclusion.

The second section of the book, entitled 'What can we do?' (Chapters 5, 6 and 7), is designed to provide a practical guide to supporting effective interventions in the Early Years when working with children and families experiencing poverty and social exclusion. It will explore the nature of our professional relationships with children and families and the various ways in which they are influenced by policy and practice. It will consider good practice in terms of 'partnership' models, which enable the inclusion of children and families. This section will also consider the challenges and opportunities in the context of collaboration with outside agencies including those from statutory, voluntary and community organisations. Finally, this section will discuss the ways in which practitioners can make use of a wide range of resources to both increase their own knowledge and understanding of the issues as well as supporting children and families experiencing poverty and social exclusion.

The decision to separate the book into two distinct sections is driven by the desire to provide a space where practitioners can explore the context in which poverty and social exclusion interventions take place with children and families, as well as outlining what the challenges and opportunities are for effective interventions, with clear reference to good practice.

Early Years settings, unless otherwise specified, refers to non-maintained settings in the private, voluntary and independent sector, and where appropriate, maintained Early Years settings, that is, Local Authority nursery schools and nursery classes attached to schools. These are pre-school settings for children 0- rising 5 years. 'Early Years practitioners' refers to teachers and non-teachers working in the Early Years sector.

Chapter breakdown

Apart from the first two chapters, this book may not be one which you read from cover to cover but instead you make use of the appropriate chapter at the most relevant time. We have included here a brief summary of each chapter to provide an indication of their content to guide your selection.

Chapter 2: Why do we need to think about poverty and social exclusion?

This chapter will begin by exploring what we mean when we talk about poverty and social exclusion and then consider why we should be concerned about children and families who experience their effects. It will consider how the experience of poverty impacts on the lives of children and their families in terms of opportunity and outcomes. It will make use of the extensive evidence base, which has located a clear relationship between poverty and outcomes. It will then move on to consider the different ways in which this relationship has been contextualised and explained and the significance of these discussions. It will clearly locate the different ways in which explanations of poverty position those who experience it and the consequences of these discourses. It will consider the 'individual' and the 'structural' explanations of poverty and the implications of these ideas. It will then consider the relative influence of these different explanations in the current context and how they influence the way we work with children and families. Finally, the chapter will offer some critical reflections on the assumptions which underpin current attitudes towards those children and families who experience poverty and social exclusion.

Chapter 3: Political and legal context

This chapter will examine the historical and current policy and legislative context for tackling poverty and social exclusion with reference to the Early Years environment. It will identify key reforms such as Sure Start, the Early Years Foundation Stage (EYFS) and the extension of free early learning places in terms of both their underlying principles and their impact on Early Years practice. It will consider the implications of a renewed focus on Early Intervention and Early Help for Early Years settings. It will also examine the connections between explanations of poverty and political ideology/intentions and the implications for Early Years settings and practitioners. It will seek to position the recent reforms in a broader welfare context and discuss the impact on the overall sector.

Chapter 4: Social, cultural and economic capital

This chapter will explore the relevance of social class in twenty-first-century Britain, examining the links between socio-economic status, poverty and the so-called 'cycle of deprivation', including the impact of discourses around the vilification of the working class. It will provide a brief overview of the historic origins of social divisions in the UK, and will consider the way in which social structures such as the education system and routes to employment continue to disadvantage some sectors of society. The chapter will go on to explore the notion of social mobility and the role of economic, social and cultural capital in supporting this. Finally, it will explore the ways in which practitioners can support young children and families from low socio-economic backgrounds to maximise this capital to overcome the barriers they face.

Chapter 5: Working with families

The focus of this chapter will be to explore the position of parents, carers and families in relation to interventions designed to tackle poverty and social exclusion. It will briefly consider the historical position of families in terms of education provisions and move on to examine different approaches and philosophies adopted to include them in their children's education. It will then examine the recent specific focus on parenting capacity inherent in the Early Intervention model. The remainder of the chapter will consider the current context for working with families and examples of good practice in terms of parent partnership models which enable the inclusion of families.

Chapter 6: Working in partnership

This chapter will explore the diverse range of statutory, voluntary and community sector organisations that can work in partnership and offer support to children, families and practitioners/settings, including an example of how one Local Authority works to provide effective family support. It also will help students/practitioners to understand the changing roles and dynamics of different professionals and sectors working together collaboratively in the climate of shrinking public services, for example, local libraries and Citizens Advice centres. Most importantly it will provide some positive strategies for the challenge of working with limited services, continuing to innovate and collaborate effectively to meet the needs of vulnerable children and their families. It will also suggest how practitioners can sensitively signpost families to the relevant agencies outside the setting. As part of this content, it will also explore wider issues of social exclusion, inclusion and participation for children living in poverty within the local community, for example, access to school trips.

Chapter 7: Resources

We know that children's learning can be affected by the attitudes of adults from a young age. This chapter will therefore discuss the ways in which practitioners can increase their own knowledge and understanding of child poverty and avoid adopting a deficit model with reference to information and resources from campaigning organisations like Shelter and End Child Poverty. It will also explore some teaching resources used with children that reflect a wide range of living circumstances. These can include picture books, which can be used as a starting point for raising awareness of diverse communities. Evidence suggests that attitudes to difference are shaped from a very early age and that all children respond well to positive images that represent a range of individuals and communities. Providing such powerful resources as part of an inclusive learning environment is clearly endorsed in the Early Years Foundation Stage Curriculum Guidance (2017) and The Equality Duty (2006). It will emphasise the ways in which a setting can provide opportunities that might not be available at home, and the importance of this in child development. It will include some examples of picture books and other curriculum resources that can be used to specifically positively represent the particular characteristics of children living in a range of home environments as a 'normal' part of the social landscape.

Chapter 8: Conclusion

This chapter will draw conclusions regarding the current context for practice around poverty and inclusion in the Early Years. It will consider the ways forward and the potential future challenges in the context of recent policy and legislative reforms and the changing dynamics of public service delivery.

References

Allen, G. (2011) *Early Intervention: The Next Steps*. Available online at: www.gov.uk/government/uploads/system/uploads/attachment_data/file/284086/early-intervention-next-steps2.pdf (accessed: 25 October 2016).

Department for Education (2017) *Statutory Framework for the Early Years Foundation Stage*. Available online at: www.foundationyears.org.uk/files/2017/03/EYFS_STATUTORY_FRAMEWORK_2017.pdf (accessed: 15 May 2017).

Tickell, C. (2011) *The Early Years: Foundations for Life, Health and Learning – An Independent Report on the Early Years Foundation Stage to Her Majesty's Government*. Available online at: www.gov.uk/government/uploads/system/uploads/attachment_data/file/180919/DFE-00177-2011.pdf (accessed: 25 October 2016).

UNICEF (1989) United Nations Convention on the Rights of the Child. Available online at: https://downloads.unicef.org.uk/wp-content/uploads/2010/05/UNCRC_united_nations_convention_on_the_rights_of_the_child.pdf?_ga=2.148671799.184432029.1496043782-1151182477.1492774066 (accessed: April 2017).

Understanding the issues

Why do we need to think about poverty and social exclusion?

Mark Cronin

This chapter will begin by exploring poverty and social exclusion, and examining the reasons why we are concerned about those children and families who experience their effects. It will then move on to engage in a discussion of how poverty and social exclusion have been explained and, subsequently, how these explanations have influenced our attitudes towards those children and families who experience their effects. It will explore the rationale for intervention in terms of outcomes for children and families who have experienced poverty and the perceived broader impact on society. It will consider the scale of poverty and social exclusion in our society and how emerging social attitudes have affected the position of those in poverty. The main aim of this chapter is to illustrate how children and families who experience poverty and social exclusion are perceived and how these dominant ideas affect attitudes and subsequently interventions designed to address these social problems.

What is poverty and social exclusion?

Traditionally, discussions which have sought to understand and explore the nature of poverty have made reference to the concepts of absolute and relative poverty. The early work of social researchers and reformers, Charles Booth and Seebohm Rowntree, defined 'absolute' poverty as lacking the resources to provide for basic physical care needs such as food, clothing and warmth. However, Peter Townsend articulated an alternative 'relative' definition of poverty, which sought to acknowledge the social context in which this experience exists and argued that:

> Individuals, families and groups in the population can be said to be in poverty when they lack the resources to obtain the types of diet, participate in the activities and have the living conditions and amenities which are customary, or are at least widely encouraged or approved in the societies to which they belong. Their resources are so seriously below those commanded by the average individual or family that they are, in effect, excluded from ordinary living patterns and activities.'
>
> (1979, p. 31)

Although it is almost certainly the case that many children and families in the UK do struggle to access the resources necessary to meet their basic care needs (the recent Trussell Trust [2016] press release stated that in the 2015/16 financial year they gave over a million emergency three-day food parcels to people in crisis, with over 400,000 of these recipients being children), contemporary debates regarding poverty in the UK have taken more influence from Townsend's definition, as it provides the opportunity to understand levels of inequality within any given society. In fact, it is this definition which provides the framework for the measures against which the UK government is required to report its progress, as part of the legal requirements of the Child Poverty Act 2010. The Act received royal assent on 25 March 2010, committing the UK government to the eradication of child poverty by 2020, although it is telling that the general awareness of this commitment to eradicate child poverty is very low.

Currently, the threshold which is used to measure relative poverty is based on average household income and states that any household which has less than 60 per cent of the median average income for the country is experiencing relative poverty. Using this as a measure, the latest government statistics for 2014/15 state that 21 per cent of the general population (13.5 million individuals) is living in relative poverty, with 29 per cent of children (3.9 million) living in poverty (House of Commons, 2016). However, arguably, the use of the *median* as a measurement of average as opposed to the usual *mean* average may in fact underplay the extent of relative poverty (particularly in light of a significant number of billionaires who currently reside here). For example, if you lived in a small community where there were nine families whose household incomes were all £35,000 then both the mean average income (adding all of the incomes together and then dividing them by the number of households) and the median average income (placing the incomes in a line ranging from lowest to highest and identifying the income which is in the middle of this line) of the community would be the same at £35,000. However, if two new families joined the community and both of their household incomes were £1,000,000,000 (one billion pounds) then the *mean* average income would change dramatically to £181,846,818.18 but the *median* average income of the community would stay the same as the household income in the middle of the line would still be £35,000. Therefore, the mean takes account of this massive difference in the levels of average household income but the median does not (especially if they represent a minority of households).

Reflecting on the current statistics in the UK it is clear that the burden of relative poverty in terms of household income falls disproportionately on children and their families. It is also worth noting that these shocking levels of child poverty have emerged largely in the last 20–30 years as approximately one child in ten was living in relative poverty in 1979 compared to one in three by 1998, a rate which has remained largely the same since (Brewer & Gregg, 2013). Some of the reasons for this dramatic increase will be explored in subsequent chapters.

The concept of 'social exclusion' is usually traced back to France in the 1970s and 1980s, where it was used to describe the process by which particular marginalised groups had fallen through the net of the French social insurance system, contributing to broader social disintegration (Evans, 1998). This concept became popular in the UK following the election of the New Labour government in 1997 who quickly created the Social Exclusion Unit, whose purpose was to determine ways of measuring social exclusion and the means by which it could be tackled to ensure that 'everyone should have the opportunity to achieve their potential in life' (SEU, 2006,

p. 3). Arguably the term 'social exclusion' became popular because it is means by which we can begin to understand the dynamics involved in people being exposed to the effects of poverty. It has, therefore, been used as a means of understanding the range of different factors, which combine to trap individuals and communities in a spiral of disadvantage such as having access to poor education, poor housing, poor health and poor communities, as well as indicating the need to tackle these issues in a multi-dimensional way. However, the concept of social exclusion has also been used to locate those people who experience social exclusion or poverty in line with particular political ideologies, which we will explore later in this chapter.

Impact of poverty and social exclusion

As mentioned earlier in the chapter, more than one in five people in the UK are currently living in relative poverty, with nearly one in three children being affected. When we consider these statistics in a broader global context it provides us with the opportunity to illustrate both the consequences and the context for the social reality of very high levels of relative poverty in the UK. The relatively high percentage of UK citizens and specifically children who are living in relative poverty is of particular concern when you consider the UK's global position as one of the wealthiest nations in the world. According to the International Monetary Fund (2016) the UK is the world's fifth biggest economy. The specific issue of the high levels of inequality found in UK and their impact has been the subject of some fascinating work undertaken by Richard Wilkinson & Kate Pickett (2010) and presented in their book *The Spirit Level: Why Equality is Better for Everyone*. In their research, they identify the income of the richest 20 per cent of the UK population as being more than seven times that of the poorest 20 per cent of the UK population, placing it near the top of a list of the world's most unequal societies. They also present compelling evidence of the impact of this inequality in the UK and other countries in the world. They found that greater levels of inequality within a society negatively impact on physical health, mental health, educational achievement, social mobility and equal opportunities. They also found higher levels of violence and poorer social relations/community cohesion in more unequal societies. Danny Dorling (2012) has also considered the UK's global position in terms of income inequality and the negative impact of this on the well-being of the general population compared with countries which are more equal. He found that in more equal societies there was evidence of greater social cohesion and trust, as well as there being less crime and competitive stress. In the context of this evidence, it seems that there are compelling arguments for the UK to strive to become a more equal society, which would require us to tackle the high levels of poverty and income inequality.

In spite of this compelling evidence of the broader impact of inequality, the UK social policy debate, which has sought to explore the impact of living in poverty, has in recent years focused almost exclusively on the effect of such an experience on outcomes for children. That is, how living in poverty affects a child's chances of reaching their full potential, with a particular focus on their educational achievement and the quality of their health when they reach adulthood. In this context the evidence is clear, as reported by the Child Poverty Action Group (2016), poor children lag behind their richer counterparts at all stages of their education, are at higher risk of illness and premature death, and are twice as likely to live in poor housing, which affects both their physical and mental health. In terms of education, recent statistics found that by the end of primary school, pupils receiving free school meals are almost three terms behind their more affluent peers (DfE, 2010). This lag continues to have an impact and, by 16, children on free school meals will achieve on average 1.7 grades lower in their GCSEs. Across almost all measurements of both physical and mental health, children who experience poverty are at greater risk, with the cumulative impact of this affecting overall life expectancy; poor men living on average for nearly 6 years less than their richer counterparts and poor women living for nearly 4.5 years less than their richer counterparts (ONS, 2015). The charity Shelter (2008) reported that, unsurprisingly, bad housing is commonplace for families who live in poverty and this experience affects children's education, physical health, emotional well-being and social relations.

It is almost certainly the case that many of those engaged in this debate about the impact of poverty on the lives of children, are influenced by their genuine concern for the welfare of these children, and are committed to the idea that all children should be able to access the opportunities needed to realise their potential. However, it is also clear that increasingly the tone of the debate has moved to a position where the impact of child poverty on the broader economic activity of the country is central. For example, the first point made on the Child Poverty Action Group (2016) website is that 'Poverty damages. It damages childhoods; it damages life chances; and it damages us all in society', which is followed by a reference to the £29 billion that child poverty costs the UK each year (Hirsch, 2013). It is telling that even an organisation which has always been a powerful advocate for the rights of children who experience poverty feels the need to make reference to the impact on broader economic activity to make a case for intervention and action on this issue.

This particular discourse has emerged as a consequence of the growing influence of the idea that childhood is merely a preparation for adulthood, with a particular focus on children as future human capital. That is, the purpose of childhood is to make sure that when making the transition to adulthood that children possess the skills, attributes and abilities necessary to successfully enter the world of work and contribute to the broader economic prosperity of the country. In particular, reforms of our education system have increasingly reinforced this perception, that is, curriculum, assessment and inspection requirements focusing on standardised and linear measures of child development, which lead to the acquisition of work-based skills. This point is clearly made/underlined in the Department for Education and Science's White Paper 'Better Schools', produced shortly before the introduction of the first National Curriculum in 1988, which stated: 'It is vital that schools always remember that preparation for working life is one of their principle functions ... Industry and Commerce are among the school's main customers' (DES, 1985, para 46). It is a point that will receive more attention in Chapter 3. This reference to the 'instrumental' purpose of education in such a pivotal government report illustrates something which has arguably become a routine mantra of education reforms. That is, we measure individual and schools' educational progress (and the success of broader educational reforms) by children's performance in tests, which are a necessary requirement for gaining employment.

However, this mantra is frequently at odds with the values of those frontline professionals who work within the education system and share more in common with writers such as Paolo Freire (1970), who argues that education should have 'intrinsic' value and be an emancipatory process, which enables us to better understand our own existence and aims to improve our general well-being. Education should be a process that is not fixated on specified outcomes but is a good in itself, whereby we are striving to generate in children a love of learning which has real meaning and application in their lives.

Reflective activity

In the context of your own educational journey, what are the key things which have had the most impact on your life?

Are these things exclusive to your formal education or school experiences?

What other things have you learnt which have enhanced your life or increased your sense of happiness or personal satisfaction, and where did you learn them?

We have to ask ourselves if increasingly stringent inspection processes, requiring us to measure children's performance against prescriptive curriculum targets at more frequent intervals and at much younger ages, are having an effect on the emotional health and well-being of our children and, significantly, on their attitudes towards learning. In the context of research evidence, it is clear that children and young people's levels of anxiety and depression are increasing, as is the proportion of children aged 5–16 years old who have a diagnosed mental health disorder which is, at least in part, attributed to the increasing levels of pressure associated with educational assessments, testing and examination (Green *et al.*, 2005; Nuffield Foundation, 2013). Therefore, a clear focus on improving the educational outcomes of children, with a view to maximising their contribution to the broader economic prosperity of society, may, in fact, be threatening their emotional well-being and mental health, which, for poor children in particular, represents a significant threat to something which is potentially already in quite a fragile state.

Why do children and families experience poverty and social exclusion?

The question of why particular children and families experience poverty and social exclusion is both hotly contested and of fundamental political importance. On the one hand, it is argued that poverty and social exclusion are a consequence of either the social or economic circumstances of the individual or family, which are largely out of their control. That is, poverty and social exclusion are a consequence of 'structural' inequalities that arise from the way in which society is organised, and in the context of a capitalist system which favours those with existing wealth and power, it necessarily makes whole groups of people with limited access to economic and political power vulnerable to the effects of poverty. For example, a child born to wealthy parents will probably live in a secure home in a relatively safe community with access to a successful school, which will provide them with the qualifications to access a well-paid and satisfying job. These opportunities will probably not be as accessible to a child born to poor parents, who is less likely to live in a secure home in a safe community, and who will have restricted access to a successful school and potentially be denied access to the education, which would provide them with a well-paid and satisfying job. On the other hand, it is argued that poverty and social exclusion are the consequence of individual failure and reflect an inability to make the right moral choices and live a responsible life.

Therefore, this 'behavioural' explanation of poverty and social exclusion emphasises the actions of the individual in a society which provides equal opportunities for all.

Reflective activity

Look again at the two explanations of poverty above.

How would you feel about working with families whose experience of poverty and social exclusion is explained to you in each of these different ways?

Which explanation is likely to make you feel more sympathetic and supportive towards the family?

Which explanation would make you more inclined to be judgemental and to advocate for interventions which coerce the parents into behaviour change?

Historically, there has been a shift in the influence of the competing 'structural' and 'behavioural' explanations which reflects the political environment in which these ideas have been crafted and promoted. The 'structural' explanation of poverty and social exclusion was undoubtedly significant in the Labour Party's creation of the British welfare state after their election victory of 1945, at a time when the emphasis was on the provision of services which would protect those made vulnerable by the workings of the capitalist system. This explanation put the onus on the state to intervene on the side of those experiencing the effects of poverty, in order to equalise or at least redress their comparative lack of power and access to welfare provisions. It was in this context that we saw the emergence of the concept of 'universalism' in welfare provision, which held that everyone should have an equal right to free health care, housing, education and social security. Prior to the birth of the welfare state in 1945, access to welfare services was often reliant on the ability to pay for things like basic health care. This period of our social history saw the introduction of the National Health Service

(NHS), free universal education and social security provisions including pensions, unemployment benefit and sickness benefits. All of this was based on the belief that people who could work, would work, and their national insurance contributions would provide support for those who couldn't work. The assumption was that people would work for the common good of all.

This sense of social solidarity and communal responsibility for tackling inequality persisted in what became known as the 'post-war consensus', irrespective of the political affiliations of the different governments until the late 1970s, and was represented by the growth of the welfare state. As outlined by Wolfe and Klausen:

> The left demanded the creation and expansion of the welfare state. Public policy should redistribute income and subsidise, if not deliver directly, essential services such as education and health. The ideal was a society in which inequalities associated with social class would fade away.

> (2000, p. 28)

Therefore, at this time social attitudes were sympathetic towards those who were experiencing poverty and there was a sense of shared responsibility, which legitimised the state to take direct action in the form of welfare provisions to tackle this social issue.

Current context

In today's society, supporters of this explanation would point to the significance of socio-economic position and its impact on life chances to legitimise this 'structural' discourse (see Chapter 4). For example, since the housing reforms of the 1980s, which famously introduced council tenants' 'right to buy' their council property, the vast majority of us are now classed as home owners, have mortgages and, in the context of the 'housing market', the location of our homes often depends on our personal wealth. Connected to this social change are the reforms of the education system under the John Major Conservative government as part of the 'Citizens Charter', which introduced the schools league table system, designed to give parents increased choice in a free market. The idea being that parents could make an informed decision when choosing the best performing school for their children to attend, as indicated by their position in a school league table.

What has emerged from this combination of Conservative social reforms is a situation in which personal wealth determines the location of your home in a 'housing market' where house prices are increasingly affected by the proximity of a successful school. Therefore, your capacity to afford a house within the catchment area of a school near the top of the school league table will significantly affect your child's access to a good education. For those children and families living in poverty, who either have to rely on the limited supply of social housing (Local Authority rented accommodation), which is more often than not located in deprived communities (due in part to the lack of interest from private housing developers due to the limited potential for generating profits and the housing benefit cap, which is forcing poor families to move to low rental properties), or low-cost private housing (rental or home owning), access to the best performing schools is severely limited. In fact, the concept of choice is only actually on offer to those families who can afford to buy the house they want, in the area they want, which is close to their preferred school. The inevitable consequence of this 'choice' is that the education of those children whose access to successful schools is limited, will also be affected, which will, in turn, place them at a disadvantage in the jobs market and restrict their social mobility. The problem of low social mobility in the UK has been routinely outlined by organisations such as The Sutton Trust which indicates, with reference to research evidence, that not only does the UK perform poorly on this measure compared with many of our European neighbours, but there is clear evidence that social mobility is in fact reducing in the UK (Blanden, Gregg and Machin, 2005).

Therefore this 'structural' explanation for poverty and social exclusion suggests that the way society operates, in this example the nature of the housing market and the organisation of the education system in the UK, presents a barrier to social mobility and therefore traps children, families and communities in a cycle of deprivation and disadvantage.

In our more recent social history the 'behavioural' explanation of poverty has grown in influence and has come to dominate the discussion. This has come about as a consequence of the combination of a sustained period of Conservative government from 1979 to 1997 (four consecutive election victories), and the growing influence of social policy reforms based in the United States. Following the first of their four election victories in 1979, the Conservatives noted with interest the work of American sociologist, Charles Murray, who published his now infamous book *Losing Ground: American Social Policy, 1950–1980* in 1984, which he made reference to the role of social policy in contributing to the emergence of what he termed the 'underclass' in the US through the provision of support which was seen to create dependency. Murray's ideas proved popular with Conservatives and he was subsequently invited by *The Sunday Times* to visit the UK in 1989 to explore whether similar social trends could be observed here. His later works 'confirmed' the emergence of a British underclass (Murray 1990, 1994) and contributed to debates aiming to justify a shift in how the poor were viewed and treated (Cronin & Brotherton, 2013).

In the two papers he published in 1990 and 1994, Murray deals with the notion of an emerging 'underclass' – a term he uses to describe and explain what he sees as the growing numbers of poor working-class people who display undesirable, reckless or even criminal behaviour (Potter & Brotherton, 2013). He claims that as the result of an 'intellectual reformation' (that took place in the 1960s, all individual blame for poverty was removed and led to 'poor people, all poor people' being seen as victims (Potter & Brotherton, 2013, p. 6). He suggested that in the UK we have developed a welfare state that effectively rewards behaviour that is fundamentally damaging to society. His explanation for the growing 'underclass' consisted of the breakdown of traditional family structure, the prevalence and acceptance of low level criminal activity and the decline of the work ethic. Society, he claims, has become too tolerant of the idea that the poor are victims, and fails to apportion blame to them for their failure to contribute to society. The young (especially those who lack good role models), he claims, are quick to pick up the message society offers that a life of benefit dependency, supplemented by low-level crime, is an acceptable lifestyle choice, especially if society does not force them to behave differently (Potter & Brotherton, 2013). Therefore, Murray implies that many of those people who experience poverty and social exclusion are in fact engaged in making an individual lifestyle choice which is devoid of the necessary moral values which is the consequence of a welfare system which facilitates this dynamic. He subsequently advocates welfare reforms which focus on 'remoralising' the poor, emphasising the need for them to make responsible choices, which are identified as aiming for self-sufficiency and moving away from welfare dependency (see Chapter 3).

This discussion contributed heavily to subsequent social policy reforms introduced during the Conservative governments of 1979–1997 and the New Labour government of 1997–2010 and which continue to provide the rationale for recent Coalition and Conservative government social policy developments (which will be discussed in more detail in Chapter 3).

The influence of this set of ideas during the New Labour government of 1997–2010 can be illustrated by the emergence of the 'rights and responsibilities' philosophy, which came to dominate their social policy reforms. As the Conservative administration became less and less popular in the mid-1990s a debate was going on within the Labour party about how much it needed to modernise its traditional social democratic values. By the time the New Labour government swept to power in 1997, it was driven by a new ideology referred to as the 'Third Way', which signalled a shift away from more traditional Labour values. Although there was reference to social justice, social policy during this era was driven by notions of developing a 'social investment state' where, in the words of Giddens:

> The guideline is investment in human capital wherever possible, rather than the direct provision of economic maintenance. In place of the welfare state we should put the social investment state, operating in the context of a positive welfare society.
>
> (1998, p. 117)

This resulted in social policy which focused on social investment with the primary aim of building an individual's capability to engage in the labour market. Nowhere was this idea more evident than in the New Labour government's significant investment in Early Years provisions, with a particular focus on early learning. The stated intention was to maximise children's ability to be 'school ready' and prepared to fulfil their future potential with reference to the skills and qualifications needed to successfully enter the workforce (further discussion of this will take place in Chapter 3).

Taking influence from (neo)liberal ideas, which define freedom in terms of individual autonomy, the Third Way conceptualised freedom in the words of Sassoon as 'the material ability to make more choices. The role of the state is to ensure that everyone possesses such material ability' (1996, p. 738). Therefore, social policy was to focus on tackling the social exclusion which prevented equal opportunity and access to the material ability to make choices. An example of such policy development was the 'welfare to work' programme, which talked of an individual's 'rights' to receive financial support if they were unemployed, provided they accepted their moral 'responsibility' to work towards re-entering the workforce. However, what is significant about this arrangement for Lavalette and Pratt is that:

> The intent of much of the policy agenda suggested by the Third Way theory has been to fit workers for capital's purposes: not to modify capital so that its consequences no longer initially and ultimately rest on the shoulders of those made poor, vulnerable and unemployed by its operations.
>
> (2006, p. 39)

Therefore, what became clear for New Labour was that to enable society to prosper and to facilitate freedom, individuals were expected to adhere to a particular model of an 'ideal citizen', which was defined by the needs of business and the economy, supported by state intervention/sanctions aiming to reduce overall dependency on the state. In essence, this 'ideal citizen' would be able to exercise their 'rights' to welfare services provided they had demonstrated that through their actions and lifestyles they were acting 'responsibly'. One of the key targets for this particular agenda, who are routinely mentioned in welfare reforms (in particular as part of the Sure Start initiative and wider benefit reforms), are young single mothers, who are deemed to have acted irresponsibly by having children too early but who can compensate for this moral misjudgement by accessing free childcare, provided they then seek to re-enter the workforce. This transition will usually entail them becoming involved in adult learning, which will provide the skills needed to enter the workforce, or they will be required to access part-time work. This is just one of many examples of how the current social policy agenda identifies individual lifestyle choices as the reason why people experience poverty and social exclusion (this will be further explored in Chapter 3).

How do these explanations affect how we work with children and families?

One significant measure of how these explanations of poverty and social exclusion have affected our view of children and families affected by these circumstances and subsequently how we work with them is public attitudes. Since 1983, the British Social Attitudes Survey has been monitoring and tracking changes in people's social, political and moral attitudes and as such offers us a critical gauge of public opinion on a range of issues, including attitudes towards welfare provisions. In the most recent (33rd) edition of the British Social Attitudes Survey (NatCen, 2017), it is reported that social attitudes towards welfare spending reflect a significant fall in empathy and sympathy towards the poor and increasingly advocate a reduction in financial support in the form of welfare payments. When asked in 2015, 'Would you like to see more money spent on welfare, 31 per cent of people disagreed with this statement, compared with 15 per cent when the same question was asked in 1989. This represents a significant change in the level of empathy for those in need of support, with twice as many people saying that they do not support an increase in welfare spending. Furthermore, in 1998, when asked specifically about whether they 'would like to see more government spending on benefits for unemployed people', 22 per cent of people agreed with this statement, compared with only 17 per cent of people in 2015. There was also a reduction in empathy when asked if they 'would like to see more government spending on benefits for parents who work who are on very low incomes' with 68 per cent supporting this idea in 1998, reducing to 61 per cent in 2015. However, the biggest fall in empathy was found when participants were asked if they 'would like to see more government spending on benefits for disabled people who cannot work', which went from 72 per cent in 1998 to 61 per cent in 2015. These trends in social attitudes were reinforced when people were asked if they 'would like to see less government spending on benefits' with the percentage of people agreeing with this statement rising from 35 per cent in 1998 to 45 per cent in 2015. Surveys such as this offer an indication of how social attitudes are shifting from a position which locates poverty as a 'communal' responsibility, which we all share, to one which locates it as an 'individual's' responsibility. It is not surprising that this change in attitudes has taken place in an era which has seen the controversial work of Charles Murray – who argued that those people who experience poverty are in fact engaged in making an individual lifestyle choice, which is devoid of the necessary moral values, and who blamed the welfare systems which facilitate this dynamic – growing in social and political influence.

The way in which the poor are perceived and located in broader society has been the subject of much debate in recent years and was the subject of a recent book entitled *Chavs: The Demonization of the Working Class* by Owen Jones (2011). In his book Jones, who is a journalist and political commentator, argues that:

> The British working class has become an object of fear and ridicule. From *Little Britain's* Vicky Pollard to the demonization of Jade Goody, media and politicians alike dismiss as feckless, criminalized and ignorant a vast, underprivileged swathe of society that has become stereotyped by one hate-filled word: chavs.

The book explores how media and political discourse has positioned the poor working class as a significant social problem and comments that 'the term "chav" now encompasses any negative traits associated with working-class people – violence, laziness, teenage pregnancies, racism, drunkenness, and the rest' (Jones, 2011, p. 8). This concept is routinely reinforced by the mainstream media whose headlines include 'Single mothers have created generation of "uber-chavs" who are costing taxpayer a fortune' (*Daily Mail*, 10 February 2009), and 'It's time middle classes stood up to "chav culture"' (*Daily Express*, 27 January 2009). These articles feed an emerging 'moral panic' about the lack of socially responsible morals and values amongst these 'chavs' and advocates an authoritarian approach to their moral correction. What is particularly shocking is the casual use of this derogatory term both in the mainstream media and in everyday conversations. It has become perfectly acceptable to label people as 'chavs' and express our disdain about their behaviour and lament their irresponsible and selfish lifestyles, which are the result of an over-generous welfare system. This has undoubtedly legitimised welfare reforms, which have sought to reduce spending with the poor disproportionately carrying the burden of the cuts.

An interesting explanation of this set of social attitudes has been offered by Lister (2008) and Killeen (2008), who observe the emergence of the concept of 'povertyism', described by them as the process by which the poor are 'othered' and subsequently labelled as 'inferior or of lessor value' and constructed 'as a source of moral contamination, a threat, an undeserving economic burden'. This process operates in two key ways. First, it locates the poor as inferior and somehow deficient in terms of the ideal or normal responsible 'citizen' and, therefore, in need of our moral correction. It also importantly secures the identity of those who are not labelled as 'poor' or a 'chav' as upstanding and valuable members of society, possessing the necessary moral fibre to instruct the immoral and irresponsible. Therefore, we are increasingly encouraged to think of our position in society as either a responsible, independent, self-sufficient and morally upstanding citizen (us) or as an irresponsible, dependent and morally deficient scrounger (them). The former being encouraged to cast their judgement on the latter (see Chapter 3).

However, this distorted picture is arguably most significant for those of us who work directly with children and families in these circumstances, as it locates us as the moral regulators with the knowledge, authority and responsibility to address these deficiencies. The stigma attached to this type of relationship between children and families experiencing poverty and the Early Years practitioner presents a barrier, which will almost certainly interfere with any reasonable chance of meaningful outcomes for either party.

Challenging the myths

Of course, this presumption of individual blame, which locates the 'us' (morally upright responsible citizen) and 'them' (morally deficient irresponsible poor) binary relationship, is completely flawed as it fails to take account of a whole range of factors which contribute to an individual's economic position in society (as discussed earlier in this chapter). In addition to this, this presumption operates on the basis of some widely held myths about the realities of welfare support. One key example of this can be found in the perception of the social security system. Once again, the media plays a significant role in its portrayal of the ongoing 'moral panic' about benefit fraud, which suggests that there is widespread evidence of poor people defrauding the welfare system. Headlines such as 'Benefits cheat mum who scrounged thousands by claiming she was single is caught after posting pictures of her wedding on Facebook' (*The Sun*, 7 December 2016) single out the individuals who defraud the system and articles entitled 'Revealed: The most bizarre benefit frauds of 2016 – including a woman claiming to have superpowers and a "BLIND" driver' (Mail online, 31 December 2016) both imply the widespread problem of benefit fraud as well as mocking the stupidity of these irresponsible 'others'. This media discourse is further legitimised and amplified by policy responses, which also suggest that benefit fraud is a significant national problem. In the recent white paper 'Universal Credit: Welfare that Works' (2010), clear reference is made to its aim to make the benefits system fairer by tackling poverty, worklessness and welfare dependency. It goes on to locate unemployed lone parents as a particular target for intervention and makes reference to strengthened conditionality, which will be supported by a new system of financial sanctions to tackle benefit fraud. The following Welfare Reform Act 2012, which provided the legal power to enforce the white paper, makes clear reference to capping benefit payments, introducing tougher penalties for benefit fraud and delivering fairness to those claiming benefits and to the taxpayer. This welfare reform agenda clearly signals the government's intentions to crack down on the significant problem of benefits cheats (them) whilst acknowledging the concerns of the responsible taxpayer (us).

However, when we examine the realities of this situation it becomes clear who is in fact presenting the most significant threat to the national interest. The Department for Work and Pensions in 2014 stated that £1.2 billion was lost through benefit fraud (down from the £1.5 billion detailed in the Fraud, Error and Debt Taskforce report of 2010). This figure is dwarfed by the conservative estimate of £15 billion lost through tax fraud in the Fraud, Error and Debt Taskforce report in 2010. It is widely reported that in fact the true extent of tax fraud is likely to be much bigger, with the Public and Commercial Services Union estimating that tax evasion was in the region of £85 billion and tax avoidance is £19 billion (Murphy, 2014). Therefore, it is clear that the cost of benefit fraud is minimal in comparison to the money which is defrauded by tax evasion/avoidance largely committed by the wealthy. However, the most significant figures, which refute the benefit cheat myths, are those which outline the extent of unclaimed benefits. In 2016 the Department for Work and Pensions stated that £2.4 billion of Job-Seekers Allowance went unclaimed, £2.9 billion in Income Support went unclaimed, £4.6 billion of Housing Benefit went unclaimed and £3.1 billion of Pension Credits went unclaimed (DWP, 2016). Therefore, it appears that more than ten times more benefits went unclaimed (£13 billion) than was fraudulently claimed (£1.2 billion), and in fact almost 100 times more money was lost through tax fraud (£109 billion) than through benefits fraud (£1.2 billion). Therefore, the real problem lies with tax cheats and not benefit cheats.

Conclusions

This chapter has sought to explore the current rationale for our concerns about the impact of poverty and social exclusion, as well as considering the ways in which these problems are conceived. It has identified the dominant media and policy perception of poverty and social exclusion as the consequence of individual failure, which has subsequently impacted on social attitudes towards levels of welfare support and general empathy and sympathy towards those experiencing poverty and social exclusion. It then moved on to challenge the myths which attempt to legitimise these perceptions, as well as beginning to consider the potential impact on the day-to-day relationships between those who need support and those in the position to offer support. It has invited you to re-examine your attitudes towards and perceptions of those children and families who experience poverty and social exclusion and, in particular, to revisit the 'structural' context in which this problem exists in terms of increasing levels of social inequality and the lack of social mobility. The following chapters will take a closer look at how perceptions of poverty and social exclusion have impacted on recent social policy attempts to address these problems and the implications for Early Years practitioners. The second half of this book will consider how Early Years practitioners can make use of this knowledge and understanding to inform their practice.

Further reading

Dorling, D. (2012) *The No-Nonsense Guide to Equality*. Oxford: New Internationalist Publications.

Smyth, S. & Wrigley, T. (2013) *Living on the Edge: Rethinking Poverty, Class and Schooling*. New York: Peter Laing Publishing.

Wilkinson, R. G. & Pickett, K. (2009) *The Spirit Level: Why More Equal Societies Almost Always Do Better*. London: Allen Lane.

Useful websites

Child Poverty Action Group, www.cpag.org.uk
End Child Poverty, www.endchildpoverty.org.uk

References

Birchall, G. (2016) 'Benefits cheat mum who scrounged thousands by claiming she was single is caught after posting pictures of her wedding on Facebook', *The Sun*, 7 December. Available online at: www.thesun.co.uk/news/2346572/benefits-cheat-mum-caught-posting-pictures-lesbian-wedding-facebook/ (accessed: 22 February 2017).

Blanden, J., Gregg, P. & Machin, S. (2005) 'Intergenerational Mobility in Europe and North America'. Available online at: www.suttontrust.com/wp-content/uploads/2005/04/IntergenerationalMobility.pdf (accessed: 22 February 2017).

Brewer, M. & Gregg, P. (2013) 'Eradicating Child Poverty in Britain: Welfare Reform and Children since 1997'. Available online at: www.ifs.org.uk/wps/wp0108.pdf (accessed: 3 May 2017).

Child Poverty Action Group (2016) 'The Impact of Poverty'. Available online at: http://cpag.org.uk/content/impact-poverty (accessed: 18 November 2016).

Cronin, M. & Brotherton, G. (2013) 'The Legal and Policy Context' in Brotherton, G. & Cronin, M. (eds.) *Working with Vulnerable Children, Young People and Families*. London: Routledge, pp. 35–48.

Dathan, M. (2016) 'Revealed: The most bizarre benefit frauds of 2016 – including a woman claiming to have superpowers and a "BLIND" driver', *Mail online*, 31 December. Available online at: www.dailymail.co.uk/news/article-4076338/The-bizarre-benefit-frauds-2016-including-woman-claiming-superpowers-BLIND-driver.html (accessed: 3 May 2017).

Department for Education (2010) 'GCSE and Equivalent Attainment by Pupil Characteristics in England, 2009/10'. Available online at: www.gov.uk/government/uploads/system/uploads/attachment_data/file/218842/sfr37-2010.pdf (accessed: 3 May 2017).

Department of Education and Science (1985) see Chitty, C. (2014) *Education Policy in Britain*. London: Palgrave Macmillan.

Department for Work and Pensions (2010) 'Universal Credit: Welfare that Works'. Available online at: www.gov.uk/government/uploads/system/uploads/attachment_data/file/48897/universal-credit-full-document.pdf (accessed 3 May 2017).

Department for Work and Pensions (2014) 'Fraud and Error in the Benefit System 2013/14 Estimates (biannual)'. Available online at: www.gov.uk/government/uploads/system/uploads/attachment_data/file/371459/Statistical_Release.pdf (accessed: 3 May 2017).

Department for Work and Pensions (2016) 'Income-Related Benefits: Estimates of Take-up Data for financial year 2014/15'. Available online at: www.gov.uk/government/uploads/system/uploads/attachment_data/file/535362/ir-benefits-take-up-main-report-2014-15.pdf (accessed: 3 May 2017).

Dolan, A. (2009) 'Single mothers have created generation of 'uber-chavs' who are costing the tax-payer a fortune, claims deputy head', *Daily Mail*, 10 February 2009. Available online at: www.dailymail.co.uk/news/article-1139886/Single-mothers-created-generation-uber-chavs-costing-taxpayer-fortune-claims-deputy-head.html#ixzz0sj0edHxQ (accessed: 3 May 2017).

Dorling, D. (2012) *The No-Nonsense Guide to Equality*. Oxford: New Internationalist Publications.

Evans, M. (1998) 'Behind the Rhetoric: The Institutional Basis of Social Exclusion and Poverty'. Available online at: http://onlinelibrary.wiley.com/doi/10.1111/j.1759-5436.1998.mp29001005.x/abstract (accessed: 3 May 2017).

Fagge, N. (2009) 'It's time middle classes stood up to "chav culture", *Daily Express*, 27 January 2009. Available online at: www.express.co.uk/news/uk/82062/It-s-time-middle-classes-stood-up-to-chav-culture (accessed: 3 May 2017).

Freire, P. (1970). *Pedagogy of the Oppressed*. London: Penguin Books.

Giddens, A. (1998) *The Third Way: The Renewal of Social Democracy*. Oxford: Polity Press.

Green, H., McGinnity, A., Meltzer, H., Ford, T. & Goodman, R. (2005). *Mental Health of Children and Young People in Great Britain, 2004*. Office for National Statistics. London: HMSO.

Hirsch, D. (2013) 'An Estimate of the Costs of Child Poverty in 2013'. Available online at: www.cpag.org.uk/content/estimate-cost-child-poverty-2013 (accessed: 3 May 2017).

HM Government (2010) 'Tackling Fraud and Error in Government: A Report of the Fraud, Error and Debt Taskforce'. Available online at: www.gov.uk/government/uploads/system/uploads/attachment_data/file/62522/HMG-Fraud-and-Error-Report-Feb-2011-v35.pdf (accessed: 3 May 2017).

House of Commons (2016) 'Poverty in the UK: Statistics'. Available online at: http://researchbriefings.files.parliament.uk/documents/SN07096/SN07096.pdf (accessed: 9 November 2016).

International Monetary Fund (2016) *World Economic Outlook Database*. Available online at: http://www.imf.org/external/pubs/ft/weo/2016/02/weodata/index.aspx (accessed: 9 November 2016).

Jones, O. (2011) *Chavs: The Demonization of the Working Class*. London: Verso Books.

Killeen, D. (2008) *Is Poverty in the UK a Denial of People's Human Rights?* York: Joseph Rowntree Foundation.

Lavalette, M. & Pratt, A. (2006) *Social Policy: Theories, Concepts and Issues*. London: Sage.

Lister, R. (2008) 'Povertyism and "othering": why they matter', *Challenging Povertyism: TUC Conference*, London: 12 October 2008.

Murphy, R. (2014) *The Tax Gap: Tax Evasion in 2014 – and What Can Be Done about It*. Available online at: www.taxresearch.org.uk/Documents/PCSTaxGap2014Full.pdf (accessed: 3 May 2017).

Murray, C. (1984) *Losing Ground: American Social Policy, 1950–1980*. New York: Basic Books.

Murray, C. (1990) 'The Emerging British Underclass in IEA Health and Welfare Unit' (1996) in *Charles Murray and the Underclass: Choice in Welfare* No.33 IEA/Sunday Times: London.

Murray, C. (1994) 'Underclass: The crisis deepens in IEA Health and Welfare Unit' (1996) *Charles Murray and the Underclass: Choice in Welfare* No. 33. IEA/Sunday Times: London.

NatCen (2017) *British Social Attitudes Survey* (33rd Edition). Available online at: www.bsa.natcen.ac.uk/latest-report/british-social-attitudes-33/introduction.aspx (accessed: 22 February 2017).

Nuffield Foundation (2013) *Social Trends and Mental Health: Introducing the Main Findings*. London: Nuffield Foundation.

ONS (2015) 'Trend in Life Expectancy at Birth and at Age 65 by Socio-economic Position based on the National Statistics Socio-economic Classification, England and Wales: 1982—1986 to 2007—2011'. Available online at: www.ons.gov.uk/peoplepopulationandcommunity/birthsdeathsandmarriages/lifeexpectancies/bulletins/trendinlifeexpectancyatbirthandatage65bysocioeconomicpositionbasedonthenationalstatisticssocioeconomicclassificationenglandandwales/2015-10-21 (accessed: 18 November 2016).

Potter, T. & Brotherton, G. (2013) 'What do we mean when we talk about vulnerability?' in Brotherton, G. & Cronin, M. (eds.) *Working with Vulnerable Children, Young People and Families*, London: Routledge, pp.1–15.

Sassoon, D. (1996) *One Hundred Years of Socialism: The West European Left in the Twentieth Century*. London: I. B. Tauris.

Shelter (2008) *Against the Odds: An Investigation Comparing the Lives of Children on Either Side of Britain's Housing Divide*. Available online at: http://image.guardian.co.uk/sys-files/Society/documents/2006/11/28/AgainsttheOddsfullreport.pdf (accessed: 18 November 2016).

Social Exclusion Unit (2006) *Reaching Out: An Action Plan on Social Exclusion*. London: HM Government.

Townsend, P. (1979) *Poverty in the United Kingdom*. Harmondsworth: Penguin Books.

Trussell Trust (2016) 'Foodbank Use Remains at Record High'. Available online at: https://www.trusselltrust.org/2016/04/15/foodbank-use-remains-record-high/ (accessed: 9 November 2016).

Wilkinson, R.G. & Pickett, K., (2010) *The Spirit Level: Why More Equal Societies Almost Always Do Better*. London: Allen Lane.

Wolfe, A. & Klausen, J. (2000) 'Other People', *Prospect*, December.

Political and legal context

Mark Cronin

The rapid expansion of Early Years Education provision over the 20 years since the election of the New Labour government in 1997, has arguably been the most significant development for the sector since the introduction of compulsory education for five-year-olds in the 1870 Education Act. This chapter will examine the rationale for this expansion and the focus on tackling poverty and social exclusion in the Early Years environment. It will discuss key reforms such as Sure Start, the Early Years Foundation Stage (EYFS) and the extension of free early learning places both in terms of their underlying principles and their impact on Early Years practice. It will also consider the implications of a renewed focus on Early Intervention and Early Help for Early Years settings. It will examine the connections between explanations of poverty and political ideology/intentions and the implications for Early Years settings and practitioners. It will seek to position recent Early Years Education reforms in a broader welfare context and the impact on the Early Years Education sector.

New Labour and the social investment state

Shortly after their election victory in 1997, the New Labour government published their National Childcare Strategy (DfEE, 1998) which committed them to an expansion of nursery education and childcare for children from birth to 4 years old. As part of the proposals a free Early Education place was to be guaranteed for all 4-year-olds whose parents wanted one, which was to be extended to every 3-year-old by 2004. The strategy was to be delivered by Early Years Development and Childcare Partnerships, which local authorities were required to set up to deliver integrated Early Education and childcare services. Overall the strategy aimed to deliver better outcomes for children, including readiness to learn by the time they reach school, and to provide the chance for more parents to take up work or training. In the same year, the New Labour government began the process of a comprehensive spending review, which would lead to the introduction of the Sure Start Local Programmes designed to combat the impact of poverty and disadvantage on the long-term outcomes of children and families. These programmes would be targeted at families with children under 4 years old and would be located in the 20 per cent most deprived and disadvantaged areas in England. Their aims were to increase the availability of child care, improve the health and emotional development of young children and support parents in their aspirations towards employment in these areas (Garbers et al., 2006).

These initial Early Years developments were an indication of a sustained commitment by the New Labour government to the expansion of services in this sector, which subsequently involved the introduction of a specific curriculum, regulation requirements and a new Children's Centre programme to name but a few. The impetus for this significant expansion, however, was driven by two key factors, one of which was the groundswell of support for the development of Early Years provision, which had begun with the Plowden Report in 1967, and the second reflected the particular context for the emergence of the New Labour party. These factors will be now be explored to locate the underlying values and beliefs which have shaped the direction of travel for Early Years policy and the provision of services.

In August 1963, the Minister for Education, Sir Edward Boyle, requested that the Central Advisory Council for Education (England) consider primary education in all its aspects, and the subsequent Plowden Report was published in 1967. This report famously advocated an expansion of nursery education as well as recommending it coming under the supervision of qualified teachers and that nursery assistants should complete a 2-year qualification. The Plowden Report also suggested that the child should be considered an individual in the context of its family and social background, and as such the early education setting should be a place where disadvantage should be addressed and equal opportunities promoted by suggesting:

> The school sets out deliberately to devise the right environment for children, to allow them to be themselves and to develop in the way and at the pace appropriate to them. It tries to equalise opportunities and to compensate for handicaps.
>
> (CACE 1967, p. 187)

The authors of this report were particularly interested in the ways in which primary education could operate to address inequalities and paid specific attention to the role of the parents in supporting and contributing to their children's educational progress. The implications of this particular dynamic will be explored further in Chapter 5 but what can be surmised from the discourse in the Plowden Report is the increasing focus on the potential for Early Education experiences to impact on the child's life chances.

This potential came into much clearer focus as a result of the Effective Pre-School and Primary Education (EPPE) project, which was a major longitudinal study exploring the effect of pre-school education and care on children's development (Sylva et al. 2004). The study collected a wide range of data on 2,800 children in pre-school settings in England who were recruited at age 3 and studied longitudinally until the end of Key Stage 2 (11 years old). This data included background characteristics related to their parents, the child's home learning environment and the pre-school settings the children attended. As the study was investigating the impact of pre-school care and education on the development of children, a sample of just over 300 children who had no or minimal pre-school experience were also recruited to the study for comparison with the pre-school group. The findings from this study suggested that attending any pre-school provision compared to none provided a significant benefit in terms of both academic and social/behavioural outcomes by age 11. It went further and suggested that the 'quality' of the pre-school provision was directly related to the extent of the benefits in these areas. These outcomes supported the role of 'high-quality' pre-schools in the development of all children but particularly in terms of combating the impact of social disadvantage and special educational needs. It also contributed to the debate around what constituted 'high-quality' pre-school provision with specific characteristics being identified which were around the nature of curriculum delivery, adult-child interactions, parental involvement and staff training and knowledge. What emerged from this study was a clear focus on the positive effect of 'high-quality' pre-school early education and its impact on both the academic and social/behavioural outcomes of the children by the age of 11. It also, according to Clark (2005, p. 80), 'points to a significant positive influence of the home learning environment', which supports the ongoing debate around what contributions parents can make to develop in children appropriate 'learning dispositions' in readiness for school (we will return to this discussion in Chapter 5). This research undoubtedly supported the further development of pre-school provision, with a focus on striving for 'high-quality' settings as a means by which disadvantage and inequality could be tackled in the Early Years.

The second key factor which has contributed to the significant expansion of Early Years services, is particular to the emergence of the 'New Labour' party towards the end of the 1990s. As a consequence of four successive election defeats to the Conservatives, the Labour Party in the mid-1990s was engaged in an internal debate about the extent to which it needed to adapt its core values to secure sufficient public support to once again govern. This resulted in the emergence of a new ideology referred to as the 'Third Way', signalling the shift away from traditional Labour values, which advocated an active role for the state in tackling inherent inequality in society by 'redistributing' wealth by investing in the provision of services for all through progressive welfare spending. The new 'Third Way' was driven by the notion of developing a 'social investment state' where, in the words of Anthony Giddens:

The guideline is investment in *human capital* wherever possible, rather than direct economic maintenance. In place of the welfare state we should put the social investment state, operating in the context of a positive welfare society.

(1998, p.117)

This resulted in social policy which sought to invest in an individual's *human capital*, with the primary aim of building their capacity to engage in the labour market. That is, targeting resources in areas which would contribute to an individual's ability to acquire the knowledge and skills to secure a job, resulting in independence from the state and contributions to broader economic prosperity by paying tax. This shift in ideology was also demonstrated by New Labour's commitment to keep to the previous Conservative government's public spending plans and to avoid increased taxation that they made in the run up to the general election in 1997. As a consequence of this commitment to welfare spending constraints, New Labour focused the attention of its social investment agenda on areas where the available resources could have their biggest impact; on developing individual *human capital*.

Therefore, Early Years Education became a key feature of the New Labour government's attempts to tackle the impact of poverty and disadvantage via the new 'social exclusion' agenda, which sought to provide a strong start for all children in their educational careers. This approach was supported by the EPPE evidence, which suggested that 'high-quality' pre-school early education was effective in supporting the educational attainment and social/behavioural development of all children (especially the disadvantaged). Clearly, the heavy investment by New Labour in Early Years Education was a direct consequence of the need to target limited resources. This new focus was the result of the necessity to reposition the party politically whilst adhering to their commitment to tackle social disadvantage.

Reflective activity

What might be the consequences of focusing resources in such a way?

Can we provide a strong start for children by focusing only on their educational journeys?

What other aspects of their needs should we pay attention to in order to provide them with a strong start?

Tackling social exclusion

In December 1997, shortly after the New Labour Party's landslide election victory in May of the same year, the then Prime Minister Tony Blair set up the Social Exclusion Unit. It was one of the first significant reforms by the new government, which signalled its intention to adopt a new approach to tackling the problem of poverty. The unit defined 'social exclusion' as:

> What can happen when people or areas suffer from a combination of linked problems such as unemployment, poor skills, low incomes, poor housing, high crime, poor health and family breakdown.
>
> (Office of the Deputy Prime Minister 2004, p. 2)

This was the first time the concept had entered mainstream UK politics although it was well established in the broader European context. As noted by Ruth Lister (2004), the theoretical roots of the concept of social exclusion lie in classical sociology and the work of Max Weber who referred to it as the ways in which particular groups in society, through the exercise of power, secure and maintain their own privilege at the expense of those different from their own members (explored further in Chapter 4). Its more recent political use can be traced to France, where it was employed in the 1970s and 1980s to describe a range of marginalised groups who had fallen through the net of the social insurance system (Evans 1998). The term was formally adopted by the European Commission in the late 1980s and embedded in the Amsterdam Treaty in 1997 as one of its social policy objectives.

The work of the Social Exclusion Unit in the UK would focus around looking for solutions, which would prevent social exclusion, make sure mainstream services deliver for everyone and reintegrate people who have fallen through the welfare net (Office of the Deputy Prime Minister 2004, p.3). Through the work of this unit, the New Labour government made specific reference to the rationale for this new approach to tackling poverty being related to the failed approaches of previous governments, who had attempted to deal with each of the problems of social exclusion individually. They also suggested that this lack of success could be attributed to not acknowledging the complicated links between them, or preventing problems from arising in the first place. Therefore, their remit would be 'to help improve government action to reduce social exclusion by producing joined-up solutions to joined-up problems' (Office of the Deputy Prime Minister 2004, p. 2).

However, as indicated in the work of Ruth Lister, the concept of social exclusion has been described in a variety of ways and, as argued by Ruth Levitas (1998 & 2000), its conception can significantly influence the nature of those actions it prescribes to tackle it. Levitas argues that there is evidence of three main conceptions of social exclusion in the UK, which she describes as RED, MUD and SID. RED refers to a Redistributive and Egalitarian Discourse, which talks of a social rights and social justice agenda. This conception makes reference to the provision of universal services and ensuring all citizens have access to these welfare services as a fundamental right. In contrast, the MUD concept is a Moralistic discourse, which locates the Underclass in terms of their Dependency on welfare provisions, which emphasises their lack of the necessary moral compass and the need for interventions to coerce them into more responsible independent citizenship. The SID conception is focused on Social Integration as a means to tackle social exclusion, which is the result of exclusion from paid work. Therefore, this conception advocates for interventions, which enable social integration or social inclusion via paid work supported by education and training. Clearly the aims of the Social Exclusion Unit did make some rhetorical reference to the RED conception in terms of 'making sure mainstream services deliver for everyone' and the SID conception in terms of 'reintegrating people who have fallen through the welfare net'. However, it is important to explore how recent Early Years Education policies and initiatives designed to tackle poverty and social exclusion have taken influence from these conceptions and the reality of these interventions for practitioners, children and their families.

By way of cementing New Labour's intention to tackle poverty and social exclusion, in his Beveridge Lecture on the 18 March 1999, the Prime Minister Tony Blair committed his government to abolishing child poverty by 2020. At the beginning of this speech he said: 'I will set out our historic aim that ours is the first generation to end child poverty for ever, and it will take a generation. It is a 20-year mission but I believe it can be done' (Blair 1999). Some early progress towards this aspiration was reported in the Social Exclusion Unit's report *Reaching Out: An Action Plan on Social Exclusion* in 2006 in which Tony Blair stated in the introduction that: 'Since 1997 we have made great progress. Over 2 million more people are in work. 800,000 children and 1 million pensioners have been lifted out of poverty' (2006, p. 3). Shortly after this, however, progress stalled and his successor, Gordon Brown, at the Labour Party conference on the 23 September 2008, announced his government's intention to enshrine this commitment into law and the Child Poverty Act 2010 received royal assent in March 2010 with cross party support, shortly before the election of the Coalition government in May 2010. However, the original aim of abolishing child poverty had been significantly watered down, with a main target now to reduce the percentage of children who live in relative poverty (household income of less than 60 per cent of the UK median income) to less than 10 per cent by 2020, which was a level of relative poverty comparable with other European countries. It is a target, which in light of the most recent child poverty statistics (discussed in more detail in Chapter 2), reporting that 29 per cent (3.9 million) of children were living in relative poverty (House of Commons 2016), looks increasingly out of reach. There is no doubt that the concept of social exclusion, as a vehicle through which poverty and its impact on children and families can be tackled, has been enthusiastically embraced by both the Coalition government (2010–2015) and the current Conservative government (2015 to date), but what has changed is the way in which social exclusion has been described and the solutions designed. To illuminate this change, we will make further use of Ruth Levitas's conceptions of social exclusion (RED, MUD & SID) as well as considering the implications of this changing context for Early Years interventions.

Sure Start and other developments

As mentioned earlier, following the comprehensive spending review of 1998, the New Labour government began the roll out of its first phase of Sure Start Local Programmes (SSLP), which were designed to 'improve the life chances of younger children through better access to early education and play, health services for children and parents, family support and advice on nurturing' (Glass 1999, p. 257). Although initially located only in the 20 per cent most deprived and disadvantaged areas in England, services were available to all families with children under 4 years old. The overall aims of these SSLP's were to increase the availability of child care (integrated with early education) for all children; improve the health and emotional development of young children and support parents, both in their role as parents and in their aspirations towards employment. The guidance (Sure Start Unit 2000, 2001) also required that the physical location of SSLP's maximized the likelihood of easy access for parents. This initial design clearly located the key role of early education for children to improve their later life chances as well as supporting parents back into work, which takes influence from the SID conception of social exclusion, advocating for interventions that enable social integration or social inclusion via paid work supported by education and training. However, it also takes some influence from the RED conception of social exclusion as, by locating SSLP's in disadvantaged areas, it seeks to address the issue of access to welfare services. The later expansion of the Sure Start programme as a consequence of the 'Every Child Matters' agenda, which resulted in the development of 3,500 Children's Centres (one in every community in England) by 2010, led to a more comprehensive commitment to the principle of ensuring that every family with young children could access these welfare provisions as a social right (RED).

In addition to the development of the Sure Start programme, other Early Years reforms emerged which were designed to support the New Labour government's aspirations for tackling social exclusion, with a clear focus on the potential contribution of Early Education as an agent for social change. A key example of this is the Early Years Foundation Stage, which was originally introduced in 2008 as a statutory framework setting out the legal requirements for learning, development and welfare for all those Early Years settings, providing state-funded services to children 0–4 years old. Although it was essentially a curriculum guide to children's early learning, it made explicit reference to its role in terms of tackling inequality and supporting children's life chances. In the introduction to the framework it states:

Every child deserves the best possible start in life and support to fulfil their potential. A child's experience in the early years has a major impact on their future life chances. A secure, safe and happy childhood is important in its own right, and it provides the foundation for children to make the most of their abilities and talents as they grow up.

(DCSF 2008a, p. 7)

It went on to state that 'the EYFS will be central to the delivery of the new duties on improving outcomes and reducing inequalities' (DCSF 2008a, p. 7). This clearly located the EYFS and its perceived potential to contribute to the broader aspiration of tackling social exclusion by improving the life chances of children by supporting their educational progress (SID). The EYFS also made reference to its role in terms of meeting the then aspirations of the broader Every Child Matters agenda: 'The overarching aim of the EYFS is to help young children achieve the five Every Child Matters outcomes of staying safe, being healthy, enjoying and achieving, making a positive contribution and achieving economic well-being' (DCSF 2008a, p. 7), which was instigated following the Lord Laming inquiry into the death of Victoria Climbie. The introduction of the EYFS and the legal requirement for all Early Years providers to adhere to its regulations from September 2008, was all the more significant when considered alongside the extension of free childcare for parents with children 3–4 years old. It was reported by the DCSF (2008b) that by 2007, 92 per cent of 3-year-olds and 97 per cent of 4-year-olds were accessing the free 12.5 hours of childcare on offer, which illustrated the potential influence of this combination of initiatives, which was drawing in increasing numbers of young children to Early Years providers (many of whom were located in Sure Start centres), and who were delivering early learning opportunities in line with the EYFS.

Coalition and Conservative government developments

Following the election of May 2010, the Coalition government, which was subsequently formed between the Conservative and the Liberal Democratic parties, published their programme for government, and in the foreword to this document the party leaders stated that:

> When you take Conservative plans to strengthen families and encourage social responsibility, and add to them the Liberal Democrat passion for protecting our civil liberties and stopping the relentless incursion of the state into the lives of individuals, you create a Big Society matched by big citizens. This offers the potential to completely recast the relationship between people and the state: citizens empowered; individual opportunity extended; communities coming together to make lives better. We believe that the combination of our ideas will help us to create a much stronger society: one where those who can, do; and those who cannot, we always help.
>
> (HM Government 2010, p. 7)

In this joint statement of intention there were some key themes, which indicated a significant change in direction in terms of the government's approach to tackling social problems and delivering welfare services. First, there was an emphasis on shrinking the role played by the government or in their words: 'stopping the relentless incursion of the state'. Second, was an emphasis on the notion of individual responsibility, presented as a counterpoint to the excessive intervention of the state, and third, voluntary action was emphasised as a key element of welfare, with only a safety net form of provision for those who 'cannot' help themselves (adapted from Cronin & Brotherton 2013).

With more specific reference to social exclusion, the coalition indicated in this programme for government that the direction of travel for Sure Start was to change by stating that 'We will take Sure Start back to its original purpose of early intervention, increase its focus on the neediest families' (HM Government 2010, p. 19). This revised focus for Sure Start was also embraced by the next Conservative government when they came to power in 2015. The consequence of this change has recently been revealed by the Department of Education, following a freedom of information request made by Children and Young People Now, that since 2010, 295 children's centre buildings have been closed. In addition to this, it was also revealed that 'there are now a total of 731 sites where services have either been merged or reduced to such an extent that they technically can no longer be called a children's centre, and have been "de-registered". This means that there are now 1,026 fewer children's centres than there were in 2010' (Puffet 2016). Consequently, the reduction in the availability and reach of the Sure Start programme represents a shift away from the RED conception of social exclusion as this development has almost certainly presented a barrier to access these services for significant numbers of children and their families.

Reflective activity

What are the implications of this dramatic reduction in Sure Start services?

How might this significant change of focus for Sure Start affect the children and families who have come to rely on these services?

What might the consequences be for the families who find themselves no longer able to access these services?

Early intervention and parenting

A further significant policy agenda, which emerged under the Coalition government specific to the Early Years sector and its role in tackling social exclusion, involved a new approach to the practice of early intervention. This new approach was set out in a report written by the Labour MP, Graham Allen, entitled 'Early Intervention:

The Next Steps', where he states: 'I use the term Early Intervention to refer to the general approaches, and the specific policies and programmes, which help to give children aged 0–3 the social and emotional bedrock they need to reach their full potential' (Allen 2011, p. xiii). He also adds that:

> Early intervention is an approach which offers our country a real opportunity to make lasting improvements in the lives of children, to forestall many persistent social problems and end their transmission from one generation to the next, and to make long-term savings in public spending.
>
> (Allen 2011, p. vii)

These opening remarks clearly indicate that for Allen the early years of a child's life are the key ones for intervention to break the cycle of deprivation, but equally he makes reference to reducing the costs associated with welfare provision. It is significant that throughout this review report, commissioned by the Coalition government, Allen refers to evidence from research and practice to support his recommendations:

> The economic benefits of early intervention are clear, and consistently demonstrate good returns on investment. One example documented in research is estimated to have provided benefits, in the form of reduced welfare and criminal justice expenditures, higher tax revenues and improved mental health of up to five times greater than its cost.
>
> (Allen 2011, p. xiv)

He further asserts that, 'A key finding is that babies are born with 25 per cent of their brains developed, and there is then a rapid period of development so that by the age of three their brains are 80 per cent developed' (Allen 2011, p. xiii). He goes on to claim that, 'In that period, neglect, the wrong type of parenting and other adverse experiences can have a profound effect on how children are emotionally "wired"' (Allen 2011, p. xiii). Allen then moves on to make his most significant statement with respect to recommended actions to address social problems when he claims that:

> What parents do is more important than who they are. Especially in a child's earliest years, the right kind of parenting is a bigger influence on their future than wealth, class, education or any other common social factor.

(Allen 2011, p. xiv)

It is in these telling words that Allen clearly indicates that, in his opinion, certain parents and their actions are the reason for persistent social problems, whilst at the same time he dismisses the influence of any broader social factors. This review signalled a significant shift in the focus of Coalition social policy in terms of addressing social problems and the intention to place parents in the spotlight. This can be evidenced by the subsequent review of the core purpose of Sure Start Children's Centres in 2011, which, in aiming to improve the outcomes for young children from the most disadvantaged families, moved from providing parenting support to improving parenting skills. This indicated a significant shift from supporting parents to managing their responsibilities (whilst acknowledging that a wide range of approaches and styles can and do exist) to a position where a particular set of skills were seen as preferable and needing to be instilled. This was to be reinforced by the introduction in 2011 of a 'payment by results' trial in 30 Local Authority areas, where Sure Start Children's Centres were to be measured and financially rewarded directly in terms of their success in relation to the new core purpose.

In addition to this, a 2-year pilot scheme was launched in the summer of 2012 which offered all parents with a child under 5 in three Local Authority areas, free vouchers to attend parenting classes. It is significant that the chosen areas had either medium or high levels of deprivation. Clearly, improving the parenting skills of poor parents was to be at the forefront of Coalition early intervention policy. This was further reinforced in October 2011 when the government set up its 'Troubled Families Team', tasked with turning around the lives of the 120,000 'most troubled' families thought to be responsible for a disproportionate use of welfare resources.

Reflective activity

In your experience, is parenting the only factor which can impact on the lives of children?

What other factors do you think can impact on a child's ability to reach their potential?

What are the potential issues around targeting the poor and the parenting style they employ in the care of their children?

In the context of the 'what works' policy development process, which emerged under the previous New Labour government, it is important to be clear about the rationale and evidence base from which this specific focus on parenting as the genesis of social problems had emerged. In his review report, Graham Allen makes specific reference to research undertaken in 2008/2009 by the organisation Demos – which was led by an advisory board on which he himself sat, alongside Iain Duncan Smith – published as *Building Character* (Lexmond & Reeves 2009). This research was based on the millennium cohort study data and utilised the data sets of approximately 9,000 households. It aimed to measure 5-year-olds according to what it termed their 'character', which it considered to be a significant predictor of a child's future success. It defined character in terms of application (the ability to stick with things), self-regulation (an ability to regulate emotions) and empathy (the ability to put yourself in another person's shoes), and looked at which factors had the biggest influence on the child's development.

The research took into consideration three broad areas of potential influence on a child's development of character, namely structural factors (poverty, ethnicity, family structure, disability and parental background), parenting style (approach to parenting) and psychological vulnerability (genetic, pre-natal and early environmental factors affecting temperament). The report concluded that parenting style had the biggest impact on the development of a child's character and its subsequent outcomes. It went further by classifying four specific parenting styles and identifying 'tough love' (warm and responsive approach with clear boundaries) as the most successful and 'disengaged' (low in warmth and discipline) as the least successful. It also identified that tough love was less prevalent in low-income households and disengaged parenting was most prevalent in these households.

This evidence appeared to provide a clear rationale for both promoting a 'tough-love' approach and focusing on the transmission of these 'parenting skills' to disadvantaged parents/those on low-incomes. However, other significant outcomes are hidden in this data. Close examination of the results shows, in fact, that income is as, if not more, significant in terms of the outcomes for children. Of the children from families with the lowest incomes only 11 per cent were in the top 20 per cent for outcomes compared with 36 per cent in the bottom 20 per cent for outcomes, a more significant difference than those of the children from disengaged parents (10 per cent in the top 20 per cent, 30 per cent in the bottom 20 per cent). Therefore, growing up in poverty had a bigger influence on children's outcomes than growing up with disengaged parents. Furthermore, of children from the richest families, 28 per cent were in the top 20 per cent for outcomes compared with 10 per cent from the bottom 20 per cent, again a more significant difference than those of tough-love parents (26 per cent in the top 20 per cent, 11 per cent in the bottom 20 per cent). Therefore, the advantage of growing up with wealth was more significant than growing up with tough love parents. The results, which located income as most significant were dismissed in the report, as it was argued there was evidence that confident poor parents could achieve as much as high-income parents.

It seems clear that the messages from this report were intended to support a policy agenda, which exclusively focused on individuals and their need to change, in this case their 'parenting style' whilst dismissing the influence of broader structural factors such as socio-economic status. This report was followed up by a further piece of research by Demos published as *Under the Influence* (Bartlett, Grist and Hahn 2011), which attempted to reinforce the significance of parenting style with a specific focus on problem drinking. However, again the results of the research fell short of establishing any significant links between the parenting style experienced by children in their early years and the course of their later life. In spite of the frailty of these pieces of evidence they were used by the Coalition government to justify a social policy approach which identified individual behaviour change as the main cause of disadvantage and social exclusion (adapted from Cronin & Brotherton 2013). In the context of the work of Ruth Levitas (as discussed earlier) this represents a significant shift towards the MUD conception of social exclusion, which locates the behaviour of individuals as the cause for their experience of social exclusion and advocates interventions to correct their behaviour, which in this instance is evidenced by the subsequent delivery of parenting programmes. It is notable that this new approach to early intervention was also legitimised by the endorsements of Dame Claire Tickell in her *Review of the EYFS* in 2011:

> Graham Allen recently published his recommendations for better, earlier, identification of those children who are most vulnerable to the effects of deprivation and dysfunction. Graham made a compelling case for investment in early intervention to prevent these children becoming adults struggling to participate in mainstream society.
>
> (Tickell 2011, p. 25)

and by Professor Eileen Munro in her *Review of Child Protection* in 2011:

> Like the reviews led by Graham Allen MP, Dame Clare Tickell, and Rt Hon Frank Field MP, this review has noted the growing body of evidence of the effectiveness of early intervention with children and families and shares their view on the importance of providing such help.
>
> (Munro 2011, p. 7)

The Coalition government had clearly indicated its intention to put the responsibility for social exclusion and disadvantage squarely in the hands of poor children's parents, whilst ignoring the significant impact of families' socio-economic position (as clearly indicated in their own research).

So, to what degree has this new approach to targeting poor or troubled families been successful? In terms of the Troubled Families Programme, following the completion of the first phase of the initiative, which originally targeted 120,000 families between 2012 and 2015 at a cost of £448 million, the Conservative government decided to extend the programme in 2015 for a further 5 years to target a further 400,000 families at a cost of £900 million. This decision was based on government claims that 99 per cent of families targeted had had their lives turned around, which was stated in the speech by David Cameron when announcing the extended programme, he said 'I can announce today that almost all of the 117,000 families which the programme started working with have now been turned around' he also stated: 'This has saved as much as £1.2 billion in the process' (Cameron 2015). However, these claims have subsequently been cast in serious doubt, as the outcomes from the government commissioned formal evaluation of the programme carried out by the National Institute of Economic and Social Research clearly stated that:

> The key finding is that across a wide range of outcomes, covering the key headline objectives of the programme – employment, benefit receipt, school attendance, safeguarding and child welfare – we were unable to find consistent evidence that the Troubled Families programme had any significant or systematic impact.
>
> (National Institute of Economic and
> Social Research 2016, p. 20)

Furthermore, the Public Accounts Committee who are appointed by the House of Commons to examine public expenditure recently reported that 'The terminology used by the Department overstated the success of the Troubled Families programme in transforming the lives of families', it went on to state that 'The Department has not demonstrated that the programme has provided genuine financial savings' (Public Accounts Committee 2016, p. 6).

What about the delivery of free parenting classes to poor parents? This became known as the 'CANparent trial' and it aimed to deliver universal parenting classes to all parents of children aged 0–5 years old in three Local Authority areas (Camden, Middlesbrough and High Peak) which, as mentioned earlier were areas of medium to high deprivation. In this primary aim it fell well short, as the programme was only delivered to around 4 per cent of the eligible families in these areas (Department for Education 2014). In the interim report, when exploring the reasons for reluctance to attend these parenting classes, there was a widespread sense that the classes were not needed because parents had support. It was also reported by the poorer parents in these areas that they were concerned about the classes being potentially judgemental in nature, or that participation in classes would be seen as a sign of failure on their part (Department for Education 2013). It seems that the assumption that all parents in areas of significant deprivation should attend a parenting class has not been effective in securing the participation of these parents and that the judgemental nature of this assumption might have been a key barrier.

Conclusion

It is clear that the New Labour government of 1997 positioned Early Years Education as a key arena where social exclusion and poverty could be tackled within the context of their new 'social investment state' political aspirations. Broadly speaking, this approach to tackling social exclusion has been embraced by the subsequent Coalition government as well as the current Conservative government. However, what we have seen is a significant shift in the concept of social exclusion, utilised to describe this social reality, and subsequently a significant shift in the design of social policy approaches to tackle this problem. Using the conceptions of social exclusion outlined by Ruth Levitas (RED, SID & MUD), it is apparent that the key shift has seen the Coalition and Conservative governments embrace the MUD conception, which is essentially a moralistic discourse locating the experience of poverty and disadvantage as an individual failure. This conception, therefore, advocates for interventions which coerce those socially excluded into becoming more responsible and independent citizens, focusing on individual behaviour change. The SID conception, which was very much embraced by New Labour, has endured and, as such, early education as a means of improving social integration via paid work is clearly still a key feature of current policy. However, the RED conception, which talks of ensuring social rights and social justice by ensuring all citizens have access to services, is disappearing fast, especially in terms of Sure Start provisions. These developments clearly resonate with the earlier discussions of the behavioural and structural explanations of poverty, which also identify the move away from acknowledging the broader social factors affecting children and families in favour of an individual blame discourse.

It would seem that none of this is particularly surprising in the context of a Conservative government, which has always sought to place the responsibility for meeting welfare needs firmly on the shoulders of the individual citizen whilst at the same time ignoring the inherent inequalities in a capitalist society. However, what is particularly worrying is that this ideology makes dangerous assumptions about those who need welfare support and increasingly advocates for interventions which imply that correcting moral deficiencies is the solution.

Further reading

Brotherton, G. & Cronin, M. (2013) *Working with Vulnerable Children, Young People and Families*. London: Routledge.

Lister, R. (2004) *Poverty: Key Concepts*. Cambridge: Polity.

Useful websites

Joseph Rowntree Trust, www.jrct.org.uk

Vulnerability 360, https://vulnerability360.wordpress.com

References

Allen, G. (2011) 'Early Intervention: The Next Steps [Online]'. Available online at: www.gov.uk/government/uploads/system/uploads/attachment_data/file/284086/early-intervention-next-steps2.pdf (accessed: 4 May 2017).

Bartlett, J., Grist, M. & Hahn, B. (2011) *'Binge-Drinking Behind the Headlines' Under the Influence*. London: Demos.

Blair, T. (1999) 'Beveridge Lecture'. Available online at: www.bristol.ac.uk/../Tony%20Blair%20Child%20Poverty%20Speech.doc (accessed: 19 April 2017).

Cameron, D. (2015) 'Prime Ministers Speech on Opportunity'. Available online at: www.gov.uk/government/speeches/pm-speech-on-opportunity (accessed: 20 April 2017).

Central Advisory Council for Education (1967) *Children and their Primary Schools: A Report of the Central Advisory Council for Education (England)*. London: Department of Education and Science.

Clark, M. M. (2005) *Understanding Research in Early Education: The Relevance for the Future of Lessons from the Past*. London: Routledge.

Cronin, M. & Brotherton, G. (2013) 'The Legal and Policy Context' in Brotherton, G. & Cronin, M. (eds.) *Working with Vulnerable Children, Young People and Families*. London: Routledge, pp. 35–48.

Department for Children, Schools and Families (DCSF) (2008a) 'Statutory Framework for the Early Years Foundation Stage: Setting the Standards for Learning, Development and Care for Children from Birth to Five'. Available online at: webarchive.nationalarchives.gov.uk/20130401151715/http://education.gov.uk/publications/eorderingdownload/eyfs_res_stat_frmwrk.pdf (accessed: 20 April 2017).

Department for Children, Schools and Families (DCSF) (2008b) *Childcare and Early Years Providers Survey 2007*. London: DCSF.

Department for Education (2013) 'CANparent Trial Evaluation: First Interim Report'. Available online at: www.gov.uk/government/uploads/system/uploads/attachment_data/file/190980/DFE-RR280.pdf (accessed: 20 April 2017).

Department for Education (2014) 'CANparent Trial Evaluation: Final Report'. Available online at: www.gov.uk/government/uploads/system/uploads/attachment_data/file/332182/RR357_-_CANparent_trial_evaluation_final_report__09_07_14_.pdf (accessed: 20 April 2017).

Department for Education and Employment (1998) *Meeting the Childcare Challenge*. London: HMSO.

Evans, M. (1998) *Behind the Rhetoric: The Institutional Basis of Social Exclusion and Poverty*. Available online at: onlinelibrary.wiley.com/doi/10.1111/j.1759-5436.1998.mp29001005.x/abstract (accessed: 3 May 2017).

Garbers, C., Tunstill, J., Allnock, D. & Akhurst, S. (2006) 'Facilitating access to services for children and families: lessons from Sure Start Local Programmes', *Child and Family Social Work*, Vol 11, pp. 287–296.

Giddens, A. (1998) *The Third Way: The Renewal of Social Democracy*. Oxford: Polity Press.

Glass, N. (1999) 'Sure Start: the development of an early intervention programme for young people in the United Kingdom', *Children and Society*, 13, pp. 257–264.

HM Government (2010) 'The Coalition: Our Programme for Government'. Available online at: https://www.gov.uk/government/uploads/system/uploads/attachment_data/file/78977/coalition_programme_for_government.pdf (accessed: 4 May 2017).

House of Commons (2016) 'Poverty in the UK: Statistics'. Available online at: http://researchbriefings.files.parliament.uk/documents/SN07096/SN07096.pdf (accessed: 9 November 2016).

Levitas, R. (1998) *The Inclusive Society?* Basingstoke: Macmillan.

Levitas, R. (2000) 'What is social inclusion?' in Gordon, D. & Townsend, P. (eds.) *Breadline Europe: The Measurement of Poverty*, Bristol: Policy Press, pp. 357–383.

Lexmond, J. and Reeves, R. (2009) 'Parents are the principle architects of a fairer society...' *Building Character*. London: Demos.

Lister, R. (2004) *Poverty: Key Concepts*. Cambridge: Polity.

Munro, E. (2011) 'The Munro Review of Child Protection: Final Report – A Child-Centred System'. Available online at: www.gov.uk/government/uploads/system/uploads/attachment_data/file/175391/Munro-Review.pdf (accessed: 4 May 2017).

National Institute of Economic and Social Research (2016) 'National Evaluation of the Troubled Families Programme: National Impact Study Report: Findings from the Analysis of National Administrative Data and local data on programme participation'. Available online at: www.niesr.ac.uk/sites/default/files/publications/Troubled_Families_Evaluation_National_Impact_Study.pdf (accessed: 20 April 2017).

Office of the Deputy Prime Minister (2004) 'The Social Exclusion Unit'. Available online at: http://webarchive.nationalarchives.gov.uk/+/http:/www.cabinetoffice.gov.uk/media/cabinetoffice/social_exclusion_task_force/assets/publications_1997_to_2006/seu_leaflet.pdf (accessed: 4 May 2017).

Public Accounts Committee (2016) 'Troubled Families: Progress Review'. Available online at: www.publications.parliament.uk/pa/cm201617/cmselect/cmpubacc/711/711.pdf (accessed: 20 April 2017).

Puffet, N. (2016) 'More Than 1,000 Children's Centres Axed Since 2010'. Available online at: www.cypnow.co.uk/cyp/news/1156991/more-than-1-000-children%E2%80%99s-centres-axed-since-2010 (accessed: 20 April 2017).

Social Exclusion Unit (2006) *Reaching Out: An Action Plan on Social Exclusion*. London: HM Government.

Sure Start Unit (2000) *Planning and Delivering Sure Start: Third Wave Edition*. London: Department for Education and Skills.

Sure Start Unit (2001) *Planning and Delivering Sure Start: Fourth Wave Edition*. London: Department for Education and Skills.

Sylva, K., Melhuish, E., Sammons, P., Siraj-Blatchford, I. & Taggart, B. (2004) *The Effective Provision of Pre-School Education (EPPE) Project: Findings from Pre-School to end of Key Stage 1*, London: Sure Start.

Tickell, C. (2011) 'The Early Years: Foundations for life, health and learning An Independent Report on the Early Years Foundation Stage to Her Majesty's Government'. Available online at: www.gov.uk/government/uploads/system/uploads/attachment_data/file/180919/DFE-00177-2011.pdf (accessed: 4 May 2017).

Social, cultural and economic capital

Chris Collett

Does social class matter?

You may be wondering why, in a book about poverty, a whole chapter should be devoted to discussing social class. Surely in these enlightened times, when footballers from humble backgrounds are amongst our highest earners, and anyone who buys a ticket can become a millionaire overnight through the National Lottery, social class has become irrelevant. However, whilst the determinants of social class are 'inextricably linked' to money and wealth (Knowles and Lander 2011, p. 65) the relationship between poverty and social class (sometimes called 'socio-economic classification') is a complex one. And whilst money is of course of crucial importance, there are other, broader resources that are denied to those in lower socio-economic groups, which leave them at a considerable disadvantage compared with others, and impact significantly on life chances. In spite of this, social class is a factor which is frequently (and conveniently) overlooked in the poverty debate. Cole (2012), for example, points out that whilst the class gap in children's educational attainment is far bigger than any ethnic or gender gap, it receives little policy attention, while Skeggs (in Lawler 2014) sees it as a mercurial 'absent presence', bound up in concepts of fairness and equality, but rarely discussed in explicit terms. What is not explicitly recognised cannot be challenged, and therefore this denial of class seeks to also deny inequality, shifting the focus of the poverty debate away from possible structural causes, to individual failings. In recent years, discussion of social class has tended to focus on social mobility and the UK's so-called 'meritocracy', but this chapter will argue that meritocracy is a myth, and that far from being about the choices made by individuals, poverty and inequality are the inevitable consequences of the pervasive social class discourse. It will explain how our society is 'loaded' towards the better off middle classes, whilst significantly disadvantaging those from the lower social echelons and at the same time encouraging damaging discourses that shape perceptions of particular socio-economic groups, providing an excuse for the worst kind of stereotyping, based on ill-informed assumptions about values and behaviour.

What do we mean by social class?

Discussions with students on an Early Childhood Education and Care (ECEC) BA programme revealed that they still thought of social class in terms of the traditional three tiers – upper, middle and working class – but were much more inclined to believe that we live in a meritocracy, in which anyone can succeed and in which class is no longer relevant. It was only when we began to interrogate some of the statistics, consider the scope of their own aims and ambitions and explore the baggage that comes with social class that most, if not all, began to reconsider.

Reflective activity

Which social class (if any) do you most strongly identify with?

What are the factors that have led you to that decision?

Talk to your friends and family and find out if and how they would identify themselves. How important do they think this is? Are there differences between generations?

Class has been a feature of the British social landscape for centuries, but is, in effect, an artificially imposed categorisation, based on external factors, that attempts to both make sense of the way in which society is ordered and maintain that order. Going back to the middle ages, social divisions were heavily influenced by the way in which the geographical landscape was distributed and organised. There were those who were wealthy and owned land and property, and those who were dependent upon working the land for what was often a meagre wage, who lived in property rented from the landowner. These groups were, for obvious reasons, perceived as the 'upper' and 'lower' class. In the middle were those of modest, but independent means, who worked in the evolving, educated 'professions', such as law, medicine and the church, and who owned their property. Therefore, social class at that time was determined by a combination of wealth and/or education and/or ownership.

The industrial revolution of the nineteenth century led to the biggest social upheaval that the country has seen. Thousands of people migrated from rural areas of the country to the newly created industrial towns and cities. Whilst the upper class remained the domain of the landed aristocracy, this period saw many more people including factory owners, with their 'new money', and those in managerial positions joining the ranks of the middle class by virtue of their occupations, their wealth (relative to the working class) and where they lived. Many of these people were 'upwardly mobile' from the working class, and were therefore keen to differentiate themselves and to protect their newly acquired position and power, seeing themselves as the bastion of what is right and tasteful, compared with the vulgar working classes.

Official social classifications, which began with the Registrar General in 1911, are based objectively and solely on occupations. By the mid-twentieth century, the working world had become more complex and the old classifications were dated, so a new system was devised by sociologist John Goldthorpe, based on employer/employee occupations (Savage 2015). In 2001 these categories were revised by the National Statistics-National Socio-economic Classification, to form eight categories which still stand today (ONS 2010).

Box 4.1 ONS socio-economic classifications 2010

1. Higher managerial, administrative and professional occupations

   1.1. Large employers and higher managerial and administrative occupations

   1.2. Higher professional occupations

2. Lower managerial, administrative and professional occupations

3. Intermediate occupations

4. Small employers and own account workers

5. Lower supervisory and technical occupations

6. Semi-routine occupations

7. Routine occupations

8. Never worked and long-term unemployed

(ONS 2010)

But all these classifications have been designed for administrative purposes, and only tell part of the story. As Savage (2015) points out, social class is defined by much more than occupation, it also suggests a way of life that encompasses certain beliefs and values. Lawler (2014) suggests that social class is an aspect of identity that is not determined by the individual but is conferred by others, enabling the values and beliefs of those who hold more economic and cultural power to dominate, whilst at the same time preventing other groups from thriving. In the UK, the values and beliefs of the controlling middle class continue to be promoted as what is 'right', so opening the way for institutional disadvantage and discrimination and 'othering' (Knowles 2011, pp. 75–76), a concept that will be revisited later in this chapter.

Social mobility and the myth of meritocracy

There is a consensus that both equality and social mobility (the ability to move from one social class to another, usually in an 'upward' direction), are desirable for a healthy society. Wilkinson and Pickett (2010) through their 'Spirit Level' research, found that countries in which the gap between rich and poor is small – even those which are poor overall – experience fewer social problems, have lower rates of crime and have better outcomes in terms of mental health and well-being. On the other hand, countries such as the UK, where the gap between rich and poor is large and widening, there are significantly higher levels of social problems, mental health issues and crime, and educational failure is more prevalent, despite the UK being one of the wealthiest countries in the world, with one of the longest established systems of education. There is a strong correlation between equality and social mobility, and a wealth of evidence demonstrates that compared with other industrialised countries, the UK also has lower levels of social mobility, something Dorling (2011, p. 48) cites as 'a hang-over from its infamously class-ridden society'. This means that those in the lower socioeconomic groups are unlikely to be able to change their situation, and that it is ever more the case that a child born poor, will grow up poor, whilst the children of those who lead privileged lives will build on that privilege and experience success in all areas of their life. NCB (2004, p. 31) warned that 'our society is sleepwalking into a world where children grow up in a state of social apartheid, with poor children destined to experience hardship and disadvantage just by accident of birth, and their more affluent peers unaware of their existence'.

For some years now, social mobility has been seen as the 'silver bullet' that would enable individuals to escape poverty, (though not, as Jones (2012, p. 97) points out, as a strategy to *eliminate* poverty), and so has featured a great deal in social policy. Much has been done by the current governing political party to convince us that an individual's ability to progress in this way is simply about making an effort, and that we are living in a modern 'meritocracy' – a social hierarchy in which the talented and hardworking naturally rise to the top (ibid.) and where, therefore, only ability – and, more importantly, hard work – matter. In 2010, the then Prime Minister David Cameron framed this explicitly, saying: 'it's not where you have come from but where you're going that counts' (Cameron 2012). And more recently, when she took up office, current Prime Minister Theresa May (May 2013 at www.eif.org.uk/www.eif.org.uk/) asserted: 'We [the government] will do everything we can to help anybody, whatever your background, to go as far as your talents will take you'.

For politicians and policymakers, the convenient thing about meritocracy is that it places the responsibility for individual success or failure in the hands of the individual and moves any discussion of the underlying causes of poverty away from wider societal structure, even though there is a significant body of evidence that demonstrates that social class and its attendant factors of birth and socio-economic background have a huge impact on a whole raft of outcomes.

For example, we know:

- The bottom 35 per cent of the population in income terms own 3 per cent of our national wealth.

- The middle 35 per cent of our population in income terms own 22 per cent of our national wealth.

- The top 30 per cent of our population in income terms own 70 per cent of our national wealth.

(Marmot 2010)

This tells us that wealth is unevenly distributed across the social hierarchy; the higher up you are, the more likely you are to be wealthy. And that's not all. Along with that wealth comes power. See Figure 4.1.

Only approximately 7 per cent of the population attend private schools. But that tiny proportion constitutes more than half of those at the top level of most professions: 70 per cent of high court judges, 54 per cent of top journalists and 54 per cent of chief executive officers (CEOs) of FTSE 100 companies, are drawn from that 7 per cent (Cabinet Office 2011).

Furthermore, both Jones (2012) and Milburn (2012) have identified what they call 'closed shop professions' – well-paid, top level posi-

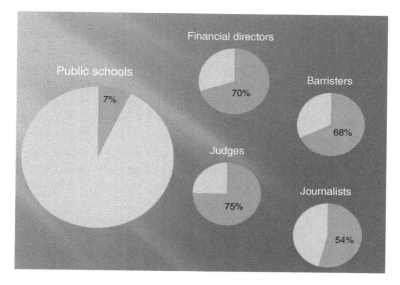

Figure 4.1 Independent school pupils in top jobs (Potter 2015).

tions, for example, in parliament, which attract candidates only from privileged backgrounds, putting them effectively beyond the reach of many ordinary people, and thus placing limits on social mobility. Savage (2015 p. 145) observes that: 'Elite occupations are the most socially exclusive'. This, he contends, is another effective way for the already powerful to maintain the status quo.

But these varying levels of success according to socio-economic background begin long before employment prospects and seep into every stage of life. Sveinsson (2010) points out that whilst white working-class boys are highlighted as failing at education, *all* poor children do badly, regardless of ethnicity. By the age of 22 months, a child with a high cognitive score whose parents are of low socio-economic status, will do less well subsequently than a child with a lower score at 22 months but whose parents are of higher socio-economic status (Marmot 2010). A child from a disadvantaged, poor background is still far less likely to achieve a good level of development at age 4, to achieve well at school age 11 and do well in their GCSEs at 16, compared with a child from the most well-off background (NEP 2010). Furthermore, 25 per cent of children from poor backgrounds fail to meet the expected attainment level at the end of primary school, compared with 3 per cent from affluent backgrounds, and only 1 in 5 young people from the poorest families achieve 5 good GCSEs (including English and maths), compared with three-quarters of those from the richest families. Almost 1 in 5 children receive free school meals, yet this group accounts for fewer than 1 in 100 Oxbridge students, and while only 25 per cent of boys from working-class backgrounds get middle-class (professional or managerial) jobs, only 1 in 9 of those with parents from low-income backgrounds will earn the highest incomes in adulthood (Cabinet Office 2011).

Clearly everyone does not have the same opportunity to 'rise to the top', in fact Lister (2008) makes the point that if everyone was to be allowed to succeed, then the 'merit' of meritocracy would be devalued. And the statistics would seem to demonstrate fundamental flaws in the notion of meritocracy. Take education as an example. In theory, if education is available to all and free, everyone should have the same chance to do well, but as Knowles (2011, p. 75) points out: 'attending [school] and achieving are not the same thing'; some children are in a better position to be able to engage with education and maximise the opportunities it affords. Meritocracy is based on the assumption that everyone starts from the same place and ignores the obvious advantages enjoyed by the middle and upper classes that help them on their way. To create a true meritocracy, we must remove the advantages that some people have (Jones 2012). But to tackle this inequality, we need to first understand what those advantages are, and how exactly they arise and are systematically reinforced.

Bourdieu and the importance of cultural capital

French social philosopher, Pierre Bourdieu, was concerned with the power relationships that exist in society, and highlighted the significance of certain types of 'capital' (or resources) as being key to social status and success (Bourdieu, in Szeman and Kaposy 2010). Economic capital or material resources – wealth and possessions – are clearly advantageous. Causa and Johansson (2010) found that in Britain the influence of parental income on the subsequent income of their children is among the strongest in Organisation for Economic Cooperation and Development (OECD) countries. Every extra £100 per month in income when a child is young, is associated with a difference equivalent to a month's development; differences that widen through childhood (NEP 2010).

But alongside material wealth, Bourdieu also identified as equally powerful what he called 'social' and 'cultural' capital (Bourdieu, in Szeman and Kaposy 2010). Social capital refers to the social contacts and networks that people develop and rely on in order to progress in education and employment. Social networking, Bourdieu says, is about those who are already powerful protecting their interests and shutting out those without it. A good example of this would be those 'closed-shop' professions described earlier.

Finally, Bourdieu identified as crucial what he called 'cultural capital'. Children and young people endowed with high levels of cultural capital, he said, are primarily those in the middle class, who grow up in an environment characterised by wide-ranging cultural experiences in the arts and sciences, and where books and reading are highly valued. In this context, children acquire advantageous 'social baggage' (Savage 2015), which they bring with them when they start school. These are usually children whose parents are well educated – to graduate level and beyond – who therefore have high level linguistic skills and academic abilities, which allow them to foster the development of sophisticated problem solving and analytical skills in their children. Children exposed to these resources, Bourdieu says, can better understand, and more readily access, the curriculum, and so develop self-confidence and a sense of entitlement (Bourdieu, in Savage 2015).

For example, Cassen and Kingdon (2007) found that a young child with professional parents is likely to hear three times the number of words heard by a child from a lower socio-economic group, and that the style of language used will be more 'in tune' with what is taught in the curriculum. Bourdieu differentiates between language-based and non-language-based forms of culture, which foster the ability to filter/process information and think critically (Sullivan 2007). In addition to these tangible academic skills is the development of behaviours that are rewarded within the education system, such as interacting with teachers in an appropriate and approved manner. Of equal importance is parents' knowledge of the 'rules of the game' in terms of education and employment, what Hatcher (in Cole 2012, p. 243) calls 'instrumental knowledge'.

Sylva *et al.* (2010), on the other hand, found that children from lower socio-economic groups, who do not have access to this 'cultural capital' are disadvantaged by the school curriculum, a phenomenon that, with increased formalisation and emphasis on 'school readiness', is spreading down into the early years.

There is further strong evidence to demonstrate the impact of parents' education and profession. Children entering primary school in 2005–06 whose mothers had degrees, were assessed as being six months ahead of those whose mothers had no qualifications above Grade D at GCSE (NEP 2010). And those whose parents are in professional and managerial occupations tend to end up in professional and managerial occupations themselves (Dorling 2011, p. 48; NEP 2010).

Savage (2015) claims that the nature of cultural capital has changed over time, influenced by factors such as immigration and accessibility to a wide range of culture through the media, and that differences between social groups now are more about cultural *engagement*. But cultural capital continues to be dependent upon personal resources. Bourdieu also recognised the powerful effects of these differing forms of capital working in combination with one another. Many of the differences in cultural and social capital accumulate across the life cycle and are visible before children enter school, through the school years, through entry into the labour market, on into retirement and through to mortality rates in later life. And in the same way that economic capital, or wealth, is often passed down from parents to children, making each successive generation wealthier than the last, social and cultural capital are also passed on so that children from the middle class, where these are strongest, begin their lives at a significant advantage compared with children who do not have the benefit of these resources. Bourdieu refers to this process as 'cultural reproduction', and so, class inequalities are compounded, bleeding over from one generation to the next (Sveinsson 2010, p. 9).

Jones (2012 p. 171) points out that this means that effectively the education system and school curriculum are 'rigged in favour of the middle class', who have the resources to maximise educational opportunities (Sullivan 2007, p. 7). Those who understand how the system works can use it to their advantage, and the growing culture of choice (discussed in Chapter 2) that has become prevalent in education, allows for 'opportunistic behaviours' that help middle-class parents to make the most of their social and cultural capital, making it harder for a privileged child to fail than for a disadvantaged child to succeed (Sveinsson 2010, p. 9). At the same time, this leads to increased segregation by ethnicity and class, as children with the benefit of social and cultural capital compete for the best schools, and those without are consigned to poorer schools (Ball 2011, p. 133).

Mass education in the UK has always been, to some extent, a means of social control. Sullivan (2007, p. 9) identifies it as 'a critical mechanism of social reproduction', controlled by those in whose interests it is to maintain the capitalist status quo (Rall 2005 in Cole 2012, p. 258). Education policy in the state sector is determined by politicians and civil servants, few of whom have experienced it themselves and most of whom will be from the middle class. Therefore curricula, policies and procedures are designed by people with middle-class beliefs and values, and will inevitably advantage those with similar beliefs and values. Elements such as assessment are biased towards the skill set of the middle class, who will be more comfortable with the social styles and interactions of the school (Sullivan 2007). Ball (2010) suggests that schools identify winners and losers at an early stage, and that even the admission policies of 'good' schools in 'good' neighbourhoods can disadvantage the poor, something which is likely to increase with the growing autonomy of academies and free schools, and even further should the proposed reintroduction of grammar schools come to fruition.

Which culture is the 'right' one?

The influence of cultural capital begins early. Before a child starts school, the 'skills' described above are beginning to be intrinsically learned, becoming 'second nature' to the child. Thus, the behaviours and characteristics of social class become part of the child's identity – what Bourdieu calls 'habitus' (Lawler 2014, p. 145). Habitus can be seen through an individual's clothing, speech, tastes and so on, and is unique to that person, but is also strengthened through bonding with other like-minded individuals.

But not all 'habitus' are seen as being of the same worth; instead the most powerful decide and dictate what is and what isn't of value. If cultural tastes can be seen as markers of status, then it is also the case that certain cultural tastes are seen as being more acceptable than others. There is a snobbery about how cultural experiences are enjoyed, and some activities are perceived as being 'vulgar'. High culture, for example (such as art galleries and museums), has traditionally been promoted and funded by the state, whereas popular culture (such as theme parks and bingo) are seen as less 'worthy' and so tend to be sustained by commercial drivers. Bourdieu (1984) noted that the culture of the working class is, at best, viewed as illegitimate and lacking in taste.

In the 1970s and 1980s middle-class values continued to be presented as the gold standard for respectability, to which everyone is expected to aspire. Independence and self-sufficiency were encouraged through home ownership and entrepreneurialism, but which denied the reality of most people's lives, in a changing employment market that left many out of work or in low paid jobs. New Labour took up the mantle in 1997, continuing to exalt the middle-class lifestyle and the values and beliefs inherent therein. Gewirtz (2010) cites the New Labour approach to parenting in her article 'Cloning the Blairs', which illustrates the attempt to shape all parents into a certain type of middle-class parent and intervening when they fall short, something which is further discussed in Chapter 5. This period saw the increasing use of 'contracts' between parents and schools to try and force compliance in areas such as attendance, homework and behaviour, many of which are still operational today. Ball (2011) offers an analysis of New Labour education policy at this time, as a neo-liberal market-driven policy in which some – those with the right values and behaviours – have 'choice and voice', whilst others are subjected to the disciplinary regime of 'normalisation'. Knowles (2011) acknowledges this tendency of the controlling class to impose its own beliefs as being 'the right way', a phenomenon, she says, that can be heard in school staff rooms up and down the country and which creates barriers leading to institutional disadvantage and discrimination.

Whilst social class can be a lens through which we can make sense of social structures, the collective feelings that arise as part of habitus, also help to create sense of 'them' and 'us'. Politicians play on this, claiming that 'we're all in this together', and by doing so, compound inequality by encouraging the 'othering' and exclusion of certain groups (Lister 2008). This othering may be hostile (angry) or sympathetic (pitying), but each can be equally damaging and prevent those who are subject to it, from thriving.

Skeggs (in Lawler 2014, p. 36) points out the obvious; that where there is hierarchy, one class's advantage will be another's loss; there will be 'winners' and 'losers'. By the end of the twentieth century, as the middle class was promoted as being ever more desirable (for winners), and associated with a particular morality, so the negative rhetoric around the working class (for losers) became ever more powerful. Savage (2015) adds that in this scenario no one wants to come last, so there is a shame and stigma attached to being part of lower socio-economic groups. During the 1990s in the US, Charles Murray, whose controversial book, *The Bell Curve*, had made spurious connections between race and IQ (intelligence quotient), identified the development of what he called an 'underclass' – a group that sits below the working class by dint of being almost permanently excluded from the employment market and with distinct characteristics, such as lone parenthood and long-term unemployment (Sveinsson 2010, p. 9). The term entered the UK rhetoric, labelling what Sveinsson (ibid.) defines as a new cultural minority or 'ethnic' group – the working-class poor.

A new ethnicity?

In recent years, when I have asked ECEC undergraduates which social class they felt they belonged to, they were hesitant. Savage (2015) suggests that this reluctance is because either people don't want to show off or because they don't want to be seen as being at the bottom of the pile. In some cases, it was evident that the students had never before given this question any thought. But there was also a reluctance among some (notably those who were more likely to have working-class backgrounds) to identify with this, perhaps because of what this might say about them. Skeggs (in Lawler 2014) similarly observed that increasingly, those in the working class are identified by others – including the media – but are resistant to identifying themselves as such. But perhaps this should come as no surprise, given that what is, in reality, a broad and diverse category that makes up roughly half the working-age population, has been reduced to a deficient 'social type' – a council estate dwelling, low-achieving, rottweiler-owning minority whose poverty, it is also suggested, is the result of their own poor choices (Sveinssen 2010).

According to Lawler (2014, p. 142), social class distinctions have been 'displaced onto individual persons (or families) who are approved or disapproved and considered as "normal" or as "faulty" and pathological'. The word 'chav', grossly misused in this context, has come to personify this group, and is a lazy illustration seized on by the media, who caricature and ridicule what is an easy target group. And with both media and politics driven by the wealthy, the working class struggles to find a voice and are effectively powerless to fight back (Jones 2012). Dorling (2011, p. 92) calls this group, also sometimes referred to as the precariat, 'a differentiated social class suffering a new kind of poverty', created as a direct consequence of wealth inequality and subject to low amounts of all kinds of capital, a lack of respect and often remaining largely invisible. Any positive qualities or contributions of the working class, who, we should remember, among many other things, built our roads, canals and railways, and brought us fairer wages and working conditions through the trade union movement, are forgotten or ignored (Potter 2015). Instead the working class is held up as a legitimate target for public ridicule and disgust, generating a climate of fear, suspicion and anger. Characteristics attributed to the working class include 'a culture of dependency' and 'intergenerational unemployment', suggesting these things to be lifestyle choices. And at a time when resources are stretched, the perception is that those receiving help from the state place an unfair burden on those who are prepared to work to earn a living and 'better' themselves. These dominant discourses, picked up and endlessly regurgitated in the media, have, in turn, led to the widespread vilification of the working class in the popular press, analysed to excellent effect in Owen Jones 2012 book, *Chavs: The Demonization of the Working Class*. Most damagingly, this government and media rhetoric about the supposed underclass helps to reinforce individual explanations of poverty, with the added effect of 'dehumanising' those who are at the mercy of the state.

The working class are accused of a 'lack of aspiration' (Jones 2012, p. 171) and the message is that those who end up at 'the bottom' do so through their own failings (Jones 2012, p. 251) and can therefore be blamed for languishing in poverty. In our proclaimed meritocracy, those who fail do so only due to lack of application and hard work, which suits the argument that the poor are poor because they 'do not work hard enough to not be poor' (Dorling 2011, p. 92), all of which helps to rubber stamp existing inequalities as 'deserved' (Jones 2012, p. 97).

Even the language indiscriminately applied to those in lower socio-economic groups (mostly, it must be said, by the media) is often incendiary, fuelling further stigmatisation and moral judgement. Hanley (2012) censures the use of what she calls 'loaded' language, when even an innocuous word like 'estate' takes on a new and pejorative meaning. And language is adapted to suit the message. In a climate of low-paid jobs, the distinction is no longer between non-working and working, it is between unemployed and *hard*-working, and often accompanied by 'ordinary' and 'decent', the implication being that those who claim state benefits are, by definition, neither of these.

Bradshaw and Mayhew (2011), however, observe that the poor families they studied 'are just the same people as the rest of our population, with the same culture and aspirations, but with simply too little money to be able to share in the activities and possessions of everyday life with the rest of the population'. Similarly, Kempson (1996) conducting research for the Joseph Rowntree Foundation (JRF) also concluded that 'people who live on low incomes … have aspirations just like others in society', but which are frequently 'beyond their reach'. Social class discourse, Savage (2015) argues, helps to keep the poor where they are. By presenting the white working class in ethnic terms, as yet another dysfunctional cultural minority, commentators can deflect attention from the bigger picture of how systematic inequality generates disadvantage while the wealthy thrive. Sveinsson (2010, p. 7) urges us to: 'look not at who fights over the scraps at the table, but who gets to really feast'. Killeen (2008) sees poverty as a new form of discrimination, and certainly the stigmatisation of the poor is directed at the most disadvantaged, who are regarded as being of little value and are denied the resources to live life in dignity. Once a 'face' can be put to poverty, once the working class is identified as 'deficient', the causes of failure can be viewed as being cultural and moral, rather than structural, and individuals can be blamed (Ball 2011, p. 178). In the case of very young children, where differences between the classes are evident from a very early age, the parents can be blamed. Traditionally the party representative of the working class, the Labour party is in disarray, whilst the Conservatives are, as Jones (2012) puts it, little more than the 'political arm of the rich and powerful', (p. 40). Both of which make the situation unlikely to change in the immediate future.

Role of Early Years: Implications for practitioners

Children's life chances are most heavily influenced by their development in the first 5 years of life, and we have already noted in this chapter that by the time children start school, there are wide variations in ability between children from different backgrounds – with poorer, working class children doing less well across a wide range of outcomes. The vast majority of 3–4-year-olds (96 per cent) in England attend some form of Early Education. This provides an opportunity for children to socialise with their peers and to learn through play with a wider range of resources than they may have previously been exposed to, and guided by practitioners with expertise in Early Childhood Education. The benefits of high quality early education have long been recognised, and will not be rehashed here. But whilst this country does well in relation to other countries in terms of Early Years enrolment, evidence suggests that the quality of Early Years services is poorer in areas where there are high levels of deprivation (Lister 2008), and that something goes wrong during the school years meaning that the opportunity presented by Early Education is, for many children, squandered (NCB 2004).

As a practitioner, it is essential to be aware of, and guard against, the negative rhetoric directed at children and families on the basis of socio-economic status, which may in turn be a consequence of a number of factors, such as employment circumstances, family dynamics or where a child and family live. It is also crucial to guard against making assumptions based on socio-economic status about differences in parenting, kinds of childcare or pre-school education, and the resources available to parents and their children. An awareness of how your own beliefs and values have been shaped should also help to identify where there might be differences and even conflicts with the families you come into contact with, which can be resolved with careful thought and flexibility.

Such assumptions about families amongst colleagues or other parents within the setting must be challenged and resisted, as must any indication of discrimination and 'othering'. It's important too to be aware of the kinds of institutional discrimination that can occur, often hidden in plain sight, in terms of expectations and understanding of family background. Even where it may not be obvious, families can be excluded by a setting's policies and procedures, for example, where it may be deemed necessary (or fun!) for children to contribute materials for a special activity, or for parents to pay a token sum for a trip. Even a special day such as World Book Day, when children are often encouraged to dress up as a favourite character, may be beyond the means of some families, so a way needs to be found to allow children to participate without drawing attention to this fact. This can be especially sensitive when a setting is in a relatively affluent area where most parents, but not all, are in a position to afford 'extras'.

It is important that practitioners have an understanding of children's experience at home, to make sure that their activities and learning opportunities are presented in a relevant and meaningful way, using points of reference that children can easily relate to. Children's interests and family culture should be embraced and valued, with learning scaffolded in a way that supports the child. At a time when the pressure is on practitioners to simply judge 'good' and 'bad' parenting (Cole 2012, p. 260) tapping into children's real-life experiences helps to restore 'voice and agency to the learner' (Wrigley in Cole 2012, p. 261). Be aware that children's 'cultural capital' may take varying forms that can be built upon to enhance learning. Chapter 7 discusses this in more detail and signposts you to important resources that will help. Genuine engagement with parents and presenting a positive experience of early education are key to maximising benefits for the child.

Cole (2012) draws attention to the current agenda of increased pressure towards 'school readiness' that will bring differences between socio-economic groups into sharp focus in Early Years settings. Heavy testing and monitoring regimes and ability grouping based on middle-class criteria will highlight differences – that are usually then viewed as deficiencies – earlier, meaning that children begin to be categorised even *before* going into school.

In terms of intervention, the emphasis has mainly been on encouraging, persuading and, when those fail, requiring families to conform to the existing system, with very little attention given to how the education system may be adapted to more fully engage with all children and families. Dyson *et al.* (2010) put this succinctly:

> [T]here has been a basic fault line in government policy, where half-hearted efforts to 'narrow the gap' have been grafted onto an inherently inequitable system. Unequal educational outcomes arise out of deep social inequalities. These are compounded by competition between schools, narrowly conceived teaching and learning opportunities, and highly centralised and punitive accountability regimes. Endless initiatives targeting failing schools and underachieving groups will make little difference unless these underlying issues are tackled.
> (Dyson *et al.* 2010, p. 3)

Added to which, the potential stigma of remedial programmes can be a deterrent, leaving a large number of children/families who remain excluded. The drivers behind such initiatives of course are primarily economic – citizens as human capital or resources who must fulfil their potential in order to make a useful contribution to society, whilst the ethical and moral obligation to allow everyone an equal chance to succeed and improve social mobility, are only of secondary importance. Public attitudes mean that successive governments are reluctant to take 'redistributive approach' to the economy and make the structural changes necessary to create a fairer society.

Conclusion

Clear evidence points to the impact of social class on educational outcomes for children and on broader life chances. Since the middle of the nineteenth century the middle class has dominated, coming to represent what is 'right' and legitimate, a phenomenon which has in turn conferred significant advantages on middle-class children and young people. At the same time, messages about the undesirability of the working class have become ever more powerful, leading to the systematic alienation of, and discrimination against, those in the lowest social strata, thus reinforcing social and wealth inequality. Early Years practitioners are in a unique position to challenge these negative discourses, amongst colleagues, parents and other professionals, through demonstrating a non-judgemental approach that acknowledges and values equally, children and families from all social backgrounds.

Further reading

Hanley, L. (2012) (2nd Edition) *Estates: An Intimate History*. London: Granta Books.

Jones, O. (2012) *Chavs: The Demonization of the Working Class*. London: Verso.

References

Ball, S. (2011) *Politics and Policy Making in Education: Explorations in Sociology*. London: Routledge.

Bourdieu, P. (1984) *Distinction: A Social Critique of the Judgement of Taste*. London: Routledge and Kegan Paul.

Bradshaw, J. and Mayhew, E. (2011) *The Measurement of Extreme Poverty in the European Union*. Brussels: European Commission, Directorate-General for Employment, Social Affairs and Inclusion. Available online at: http://php.york.ac.uk/inst/spru/pubs/1914/ (accessed: May 2017).

Cameron D. (2012) cited at www.spectator.co.uk/2016/06/camerons-sinister-purge-of-the-posh/# (accessed: May 2017).

Cassen, R. and Kingdon, G. (2007) 'Tackling Low Educational Achievement'. York: Rowntree Foundation. Available online at: www.jrf.org.uk/sites/default/files/jrf/migrated/files/2063-education-schools-achievement.pdf (accessed: May 2017).

Causa, O. and Johansson, A. (2010) 'Intergenerational Social Mobility in OECD Countries*', *OECD Journal: Economic Studies*, Vol. 2010. Available online at: www.oecd.org/eco/labour/49849281.pdf (accessed: April 2017).

Cole, M. (ed.) (2012) (3rd Edition) *Education, Equality and Human Rights: Issues of Gender, 'Race', Sexuality, Disability and Social Class*. London: Routledge.

Dorling, D. (2011) *The No-Nonsense Guide to Equality*. London: New Internationalist Publications.

Dyson, A., Goldrick, S., Jones, L. and Kerr, K. (2010) 'Equity in Education: Creating a Fairer Education System: A Manifesto for the Reform of Education in England'. Available online at: http://hummedia.manchester.ac.uk/institutes/cee/equity_in_education.pdf (accessed May 2017).

Gewirz, S. (2010) 'Cloning the Blairs: New Labour's Programme for the Re-socialization of Working-Class Parents'. Available online at http://dx.doi.org/10.1080/02680930110054353 (accessed: November 2016).

Hanley, L. (2012) (2nd Edition) *Estates: An Intimate History*. London: Granta Books.

Jones, O. (2012) *Chavs: The Demonization of the Working Class*. London: Verso.

Kempson, E. (1996) 'Life on a Low Income' Available online at www.jrf.org.uk/report/life-low-income (accessed: April 2016).

Killeen, D. (2008) *Is Poverty in the Uk a Denial of People's Human Rights?* York: JRF Publications.

Knowles, G. and Lander, V. (2011) *Diversity, Equality and Achievement in Education*. London. Sage.

Lawler, S. (2014) (2nd Edition) *Identity: Sociological Perspectives*. Cambridge. Polity Press.

Lister, R. (2008) 'Povertyism and 'Othering': Why they matter'. A talk by Prof Ruth Lister at the conference on 'Challenging Povertyism', 17 October 2008.

Marmot, M. (2010) *The Marmot Review*. Available online at http://www.ncb. org.uk/media/42195/marmotreview_vssbriefing.pdf.

Milburn, A. (2012) 'Foreword and Summary', in 'Fair Access to Professional Careers: A Progress Report by the Independent Reviewer on Social Mobility and Child Poverty'. Available online at www.gov.uk/government/uploads/ system/uploads/attachment_data/file/61090/IR_FairAccess_acc2.pdf (accessed: October 2016).

National Children's Bureau (2004) Greater Expectations: Raising aspirations for our children. National Children's Bureau Publications.

National Equality Panel (NEP) (2010) An Anatomy of Economic Inequality in the UK. Centre for Analysis on Social Exclusion.

Office for National Statistics (2010) at: www.ons.gov.uk/methodology/clas-sificationsandstandards/otherclassifications/thenationalstatisticssocioeco-nomicclassificationnssecrebasedonsoc2010 (accessed: March 2017).

Potter, T. (2015) 'Social Class' presentation (unpublished).

Savage, M. (2015) *Social Class in the 21st Century*. London: Penguin Random House.

Sullivan, A. (2007) 'Cultural Capital, Cultural Knowledge and Ability'. Socio-logical Research online 12(6). Available online at www.socresonline.org.uk/ 12/6/1/html (accessed: April 2017).

Sveinsson, K. P. (2010) 'The White Working Class and Multiculturalism: is there space for a progressive agenda?' in K. P. Sveinsson (ed.) *Who Cares About The White Working Class*. London. Runnymede Trust, pp. 3–6.

Sylva, K., Melhuish, E., Sammons, P., Siraj-Blatchford, I. and Taggart, B. (eds.). (2010) *Early Childhood Matters: Evidence from the Effective Pre-School and Primary Education Project*. London: Routledge.

Szeman, I. and Kaposy T. (eds.) (2010) *Cultural Theory: An Anthology*. Oxford. Wiley-Blackwell.

The Cabinet Office (2011) 'Opening Doors, Breaking Barriers: A Strategy for Social Mobility'. Available online at www.cabinetoffice.gov.uk (accessed: April 2017).

Wilkinson, R. and Pickett, K. (2010) *The Spirit Level: Why Equality is Better for Everyone*. London. Penguin.

Wrigley, T. (2009) 'Rethinking Education in the Era of Globalization' in Hill, D. (ed.) *Contesting Neoliberal Education*. London: Routledge, pp. 61–82.

What can we do?

Working with families

Karen Argent and Mark Cronin

The focus of this chapter will be to explore the position of parents, carers and families in relation to interventions designed to tackle poverty and social exclusion. It will briefly consider the historical position of families in terms of education provisions and move on to examine different approaches and philosophies adopted to include them in their children's education. The chapter will then consider the current context for working with families with reference to examples of good practice in terms of parent partnership models which enable the inclusion of families.

Before embarking on discussions around how we work with families, we must begin by considering or reconsidering what we mean when we talk about children's 'families'. As noted by Brotherton and McGillivray (2010) the UK has seen significant social change in the past 50 years in relation to family life associated with divorce, single parenthood and the increasing prevalence of reconstituted families (families where children who are the offspring of one parent are living with other children who are the offspring of the parent's partner). They go on to state that 'the UK has become an increasingly diverse society with migrants coming from all over the world. Many of these groups bring a range of cultural perspectives on family "values", family structure and family roles' (Brotherton and McGillivray 2010, p. 18). Therefore, it is clear that it is no longer helpful to think or talk about families in a normative way, i.e. assuming that children's families consist primarily of the birth parents with which they live. If we are going to develop meaningful relationships with children's families we must learn to understand and appreciate the wide range of ways these units may be organised. That is, children may well be living with their birth parents, step-parents, grandparents, wider birth family members, foster carers/residential carers who they consider to be members of their families. However, there may also be family friends, neighbours and members of the wider community who play a pivotal role in the life of the child, whom we must consider when working with their family; acknowledged and illustrated by Bronfenbrenner. See Figure 5.1.

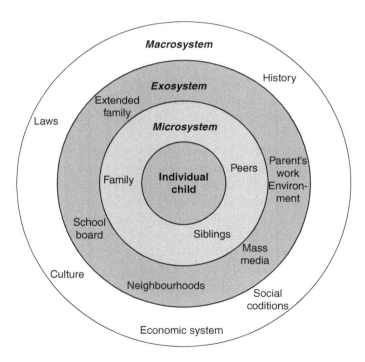

Figure 5.1 Brofenbrenner's ecological environment model.

Reflective activity

Think about what your family looks like and what it would look like if you were to draw a picture to represent it. Now think about whether those people you work with would be able to name these people? Getting the children to draw a picture of their families might be a good starting point for considering who we need to try to engage with if we committed to working with families.

Context for working with families in the Early Years

As mentioned in Chapter 3, the *Plowden Report*, published in 1967 (CACE 1967), was a significant review of primary education that was influential in shaping both the design and philosophy of the early education provision which it sought to expand. It advocated for early education settings to be places where disadvantage should be addressed and equal opportunities promoted. It also importantly suggested that the child should be considered an individual in the context of its family and social background. This was significant in that it acknowledged the unique and individual experiences of each child and the requirement to take account of this in meeting their needs. However, it also made very explicit reference to the key role played by parents in both preparing the child for their formal education and the importance of parental encouragement in the child's educational success. In the first volume of the report under Chapter 3, entitled 'The Children and Their Environment', they detailed how much parents influence children's achievements at school by focusing on the attitudes of different groups of parents to their children's education. They concluded this chapter by stating that 'Our findings can give hope to the school, to interested parents, and to those responsible for educational policy' (CACE 1967, p. 36). In this statement, they were differentiating those parents who are perceived to be interested in their children's education (and offer them encouragement) from those parents who are not interested (and therefore do not encourage their children). In the following chapter of the same report entitled 'Participation by Parents' they detail the ways in which the school should work in partnership with parents to influence their attitudes to maximise the potential of parental encouragement to improve the educational performance of the children. The clear focus being on changing parents' attitudes to ensure that they are adequately positioned to offer their children the required support.

Good and bad parents

The explicit reference to 'interested parents' in the Plowden Report (CACE 1967) has arguably contributed to the emergence of a discourse which describes or conceptualises the attitudes, attributes or behaviours which locate the 'good parent' and, conversely, the absence of these which locates the 'bad parent'. According to Sharp, Green and Lewis (1975) there are four key dimensions of the 'good parent' role as identified by the school which are:

- The good parent needs to be knowledgeable about the way the school operates and its ideology of education.

- There must be a strong interest in the education of their children and a motivation for them to succeed.

- The parent has to be capable of cueing into the teachers' interpretation schemes, in particular the teachers' definition of the 'good parent'.

- The parent has to be good at impression management and must be both willing and able to play up to the teachers' view of the 'good parent'.

The more any of these dimensions are missing, the more likely it is that the relationship with the school will become negative and the 'bad parent' label will be applied they argue. In this context, what emerges is a compensatory model of interaction between the early education setting and the parent/carer. That is, the professional will judge the actions and attitudes of the parent/carer against this 'good parent' model and identify any incongruence as a deficit in them and seek ways to address this perceived issue/problem.

Case study

Jamie is a 4-year-old boy who just started in the school's nursery provision in March and attends just one full day a week (some way short of the 15 hours free entitlement). His mother explained to the staff that she feels he can learn more from her at home than he could if he attended the nursery more. She has also recently been confirming with the staff that she doesn't have to start him in reception until after his fifth birthday which is in February. Jamie is an inquisitive, confident boy but he needs a lot of help with his self-care skills and the staff have to help with his toileting and dressing. The staff have tried to speak to mum about this but she is either too busy to arrange a meeting or when they do have time to chat she dominates the conversation with questions about what they have done with Jamie in nursery and why. Routine opportunities to talk to mum are frustrated by the fact that a number of different family members drop off and pick up Jamie and as such they rarely see mum during these times. The nursery has arranged a couple of trips for the children, which they feel will complement the children's learning, but on both occasions mum has decided to keep Jamie at home on these days (even though they have been arranged for the day that Jamie would normally attend). The staff are concerned that Jamie will not be school ready when he enters reception either in terms of his self-care or his literacy and numeracy skills.

What impression might be forming about Jamie's carer in the Early Years Education setting? How might the concepts of the 'good' and 'bad' parent be operating in this scenario? Might there be any other explanations for the carer's behaviour?

There are, of course, some considerable implications for the child, parent/carer and Early Years practitioner in terms of the operation of this compensatory model and the subsequent process of labelling which it arguably enables. First, it encourages Early Years practitioners to make judgements about parents/carers based on very little understanding of the child's family circumstances. In the absence of broader contextual information, which might take into account, for example, the work commitments, beliefs/values and life experiences of families, we may make the assumption that if they are not adhering to our perception of early education then they are not interested in, or supportive of, their children's education. Second, we do not appreciate the inherent imbalance in power in these exchanges between Early Years Education practitioners who set/reinforce the parameters for defining 'good' and 'bad' parents and those who are subject to these labels. Finally, we do not appreciate that acquiring the desirable 'good' parent impression might be easier for some than others. Those parents who share the same social or cultural background as the teachers might find it easier to understand their expectations and subsequently act accordingly (see also Chapter 4). Some parents might have the luxury of free time or flexibility in their work patterns, which might enable them to offer to support the school by volunteering or certainly aid them in getting their children regularly to school on time. These are privileges which are most likely afforded to parents who are relatively wealthy compared to those who are socially excluded or experiencing poverty.

Parental partnership

In the past 20 years there have been numerous attempts to reshape the relationships between practitioners in Early Education settings and parents/carers/families. The 'Supporting Families' (Home Office 1998) policy document was an early indication of the New Labour government's intention to pay more attention to the key role played by parents and families in their children's outcomes. This was followed shortly after by the introduction of the Sure Start programme, which placed parental involvement at the centre of its design, emphasising the importance of working in partnership with parents to meet the programme aims of improving the early learning and health of children. This focus on parental involvement and working in partnership was validated by the Effective Pre-School and Primary Education (EPPE) research, which found that in terms of high quality Early Years Education provision:

> The most effective settings shared child-related information between parents and staff, and parents were often involved in decision making about their child's learning programme. There were more intellectual gains for children in centres that encouraged high levels of parental involvement.
>
> (Sylva *et al.* 2004, p. 6)

The importance of parental partnership was further embedded in policy by the Early Years Foundation Stage (EYFS), which stated one of its central principles and aims was to 'create partnerships between parents and professionals' (DCSF 2008, p. 7). This reflected the legal requirements as set out in the Childcare Act 2006, which emphasised the importance of working in partnership with parents. This emphasis on partnerships with parents was reiterated in both the *Tickell Review* of the EYFS (2011) and the subsequent revised EYFS (DfE 2012). It is evident that there has been a renewed interest in the relationships between parents/families and Early Years Education practitioners, but what does parental partnership mean and how is it different from the compensatory or deficit model discussed earlier? In essence, parental partnership reconceptualises the relationship between the practitioner and the parent/family. It views parents as co-educators and stresses the importance of shared purpose. It places value on what the parents can contribute to the child's holistic learning and development and seeks to redress the power imbalance by encouraging parents to play an active role in their children's formal education. In this relationship parents are encouraged to take part in the planning and delivery (where appropriate) of their child's education, a model which acknowledges the value of the resources/experiences which parents and families can bring.

Benefits of parental partnership

There are many benefits of this approach for Early Years Education practitioners as it opens up a whole new range of potential resources which can be accessed to enhance the children's education. It is inevitable that welcoming the contribution of children's family members to the setting will result in new ideas and approaches to the children's learning, which might include accessing rich social and cultural insights. Making the space to build these relationships with parents and families will almost certainly lead to a greater understanding of the children's lives which can be incorporated into planning and preparation of appropriate activities. This process will challenge stereotypes and result in a greater understanding for the practitioner of the diversity of experiences and lifestyles of the children in the setting. The presence of parents/family members in the setting could also result in smoother transitions and a greater level of self-esteem and self-confidence in the children, which would clearly be of benefit to the practitioner.

There are also many potential benefits for the parents/families as a consequence of such partnerships. It will almost certainly provide the parents with a greater insight into the nature of their children's formal learning and the rationale for its design and implementation. It would provide opportunities to improve their relationship with the practitioners, which would foster better communication and the sharing of important information about the child both inside and outside of the setting. The parents would also be able to see that the better the practitioner understands their child, the happier their child is likely to be. The parents might welcome a different perspective on their child and strategies for supporting their development. This experience might also result in improved self-esteem and self-confidence for the parents as well as opening up opportunities for their potential future career prospects. Involvement in parent forums of school committees might widen support networks and reduce social isolation.

There are of course obvious benefits for the children as a consequence of this partnership approach. It is much more likely that the key people will have a clearer and more holistic understanding of their lives and as such be better able to meet their needs. This will almost certainly have a positive effect on their happiness as well as their educational progress. Difficult and potentially stressful incidences can be mediated and managed sensitively when effective relationships are established which facilitate good communication.

Barriers to parental partnership

There are of course some challenges associated with this way of working, which can interfere with realising the benefits as detailed above. From the practitioners' point of view, they might find it hard to accept the views of parents/families especially if those views challenge the expertise that has been acquired through professional training. This is especially difficult in the context of increasing levels of accountability and performance management which practitioners are subjected to as a consequence of Ofsted inspections and the school league table system. The parents may find it hard to summon the confidence to enter this unfamiliar environment, especially if they have negative memories of their own Early Years' experience. They may also question whether they have anything of value to offer the highly trained practitioner in the delivery of their children's education. There may also be some resistance from the children who may be anxious about their parents and practitioners sharing information with each other, which may alter the good impressions that they have worked hard to develop and maintain. Finally, there are some broader issues which may interfere with the development of partnership working. For the practitioner it is an issue of resources; when do they have the time to create the conditions for this relationship to develop? For the parents, it is also a question of time and whether they can realistically commit themselves to developing and maintaining this partnership around their work and personal lives.

Reflective activity

Does your setting engage in parental partnership? If so, what have been the key components for its success? If not, what would need to change to create the conditions for partnerships with parents/families to develop?

Working in partnership with all parents, carers and their families is a mark of an effective Early Years setting, but achieving this is not easy for the reasons already discussed. With the best will in the world, it is often difficult to find time and space to ensure that everyone feels valued and included and it is often the parents who are sometimes described as 'hard to reach' that would benefit from a more positive relationship with staff in a school or other education setting. Forming a constructive long-lasting relationship between parents and practitioners requires effort on both sides. Crowley and Wheeler (2014, p. 230) make the important point that there may be anxieties on both sides, and cite the *Nutbrown Review* (2012) that called for more initial and continued professional training about doing this well: 'having impressive knowledge of child development and ability to identify and support a child will count for little if that information cannot be shared effectively with parents and carers'.

There is also a difference between mere 'involvement' and 'participation', which implies parents as passively fitting into the mould set by the school, and 'parental partnership', which should be a more equal and balanced relationship where both exchange and share information about the child. Mukherji and Mummery (2014, p. 248) cite MacNaughton and Hughes (2003) who take this definition still further by 'identifying three different sorts of parental partnerships:

- *Conforming* to traditional power relationships; where the practitioner is held to be the professional expert and has the most power in the relationship.

- *Reforming* power relationships; where the relationship is more equal and power is shared between practitioner and parent.

- *Transforming* power relationships; where parents hold the power, and are involved in much of the decision making in the setting ...'

It may be useful to think about these as a measure of working with parents when reflecting on how well a setting is committed to establishing a partnership. For an in depth and very practical take on how parents and staff can work together to collaborate and share their concerns, I would strongly recommend reading another book by MacNaughton and Hughes (2011), *Parents and Professionals in Early Childhood Settings,* which offers a wealth of interesting research-based evidence on this complex subject. As already discussed, Sharpe, Green and Lewis (1975) identified a long time ago that 'good' parents in a school need to feel confident in order to be able to feel part of a community and to be acknowledged positively by the school staff. One might hope that all educational settings would find ways to make this happen for the interests of everyone involved, but it does take commitment. Some years ago, I was fortunate to hear a fascinating lecture given by Peter Moss from The Institute of Education, titled 'The Stories we tell about Early Childhood Education', in which he discussed the way in which the move towards measuring the quality of everything on offer in an educational setting, including the extent to which parental partnership is achieved, via Ofsted and other regulatory influences, can be very superficial. He suggested a different emphasis would enthuse and inspire parents to better participate in their child's education and thereby provide them with a vested interest in making educational settings more democratic and relevant. Making reference to the work of Keri Facer (2011), he described this as a 'future building school':

> The future-building school acts as a powerful platform within the community for creating a conversation about the future. It brings together students, parents, grandparents, community organizations and staff to ask what sorts of future are in development for the school's community, and to examine what alternative futures for their students and their neighbourhoods they might seek to create...
>
> [Such schools act] as a powerful democratic resource and public space that allows its young people and communities to contest the visions of the future that they are being presented with, and to work together through the spaces of traditional and emergent democratic practice, to fight for viable futures for all.
>
> (Moss 2013)

This struck me as an interesting way to think about the extent to which parents and families living with the effects of poverty might be better included in any educational setting, and how such an experience, in line with the 'transformative' definition posed by MacNaughton and Hughes (2003), might have an impact on their lives.

However, many parents, especially those from poorer backgrounds, have always felt rather intimidated and disempowered by the officialdom of schools in particular, sometimes because of their own unhappy childhood memories (Wrigley 2012). It is still a challenge for schools to make all parents feel welcome – and the necessary changes in safeguarding procedures over the past few decades, whereby physical barriers and permissions to enter and spend time on the premises have not helped this, in my view. There has also been a shift in expectations about what good parenting looks like, fuelled by some parts of the media, and this can mean that bringing up a young child is fraught with concerns from pregnancy onwards. Parenting courses are offered in many settings as a way of helping parents of young children to be more confident with varying results and implications (Odene 2017). Once a child enters mandatory schooling, there are additional pressures because being a 'good' school parent in the twenty-first century becomes ever more complicated and so can be another source of anxiety. Parents are now expected to be able to interpret Ofsted ratings when making their initial school choices and to consider the consequences of making the 'wrong' choice. The concept of 'school readiness' has also been added into the mix so that starting formal schooling can be tied into worries about whether a child is going to cope well enough with the demands of the ever-changing curriculum.

One of the best pieces of ethnographic research about how parents can feel excluded because they don't really understand what is required of them when their child starts school is written about in *Starting School – Young Children Learning Cultures* by Liz Brooker (2002). Her research participants were 16 reception class children starting school in September 1997 with varied backgrounds in a mixed multicultural community. Several were from families affected by relative poverty as a result of unemployment, domestic upheaval and homelessness, and she was interested to find out how they and their parents coped with the first year of school:

> None of the families in this group experience extreme poverty. All had a TV and video, fridge and phone, and many had access to a car at some time in the year. Nevertheless, for some families the shortage of money is such a central, energy-consuming issue in their lives that it constrains all their options.
>
> (Brooker 2002, p. 27)

This is an important point for Early Years practitioners to remember because similar circumstances can overshadow everything and so may have ongoing consequences for how parents relate to the school. One mother included in the research becomes completely overwhelmed with her problems:

> After Christmas, the family's finances worsen rapidly, and a great deal of June's week is spent appeasing or avoiding the housing department, the rent collector and various other debtors. By the middle of the summer term the family is fearful of eviction, and when their (uninsured) fridge freezer breaks down during a brief hot spell, they are unable to retrieve their deteriorating food supply, and are obliged to shop for every meal in turn.
>
> (Brooker 2002, p. 28)

This author also makes the point that most practitioners judge parent's capabilities based on what they observe them doing when on the premises and that it is difficult for them to 'conceive of the mountain of *invisible* investment made by parents, in comparison with the visible molehill' (Brooker 2002, p. 119).

Despite the challenges, there are many examples of how a good model of parental partnership can be achieved for the benefit of all involved, particularly in non-statutory Early Years settings that work with parents of children under five. Many practitioners will be familiar with training materials and resources produced by the Parents, Early Years and Learning (PEAL) project, which was originally commissioned by the Department of Education and Skills (2005–09). Another one of the most highly regarded models of the parent partnership is known as 'The Pen Green Loop', which was first developed at the Pen Green Nursery Centre in Corby (Whalley and Dennison 2007). This is built around the idea that ongoing communication between practitioners and parents, as a result of observing children's development and interests at home and the nursery, can help both to identify how to help move them to 'next steps'. It is a model that can also be used in schools and a version of this may underpin good practice, although it does rely on time and commitment. A recent conversation with the head teacher of a small primary school in the West Midlands indicated that every prospective parent should be entitled to the following:

- A personalised letter welcoming the child.
- An individual unhurried tour around the school.
- A pre-arranged home visit by the reception class teacher plus another member of staff.
- An invitation to a welcome meeting to talk about curriculum and other expectations with the opportunity to ask questions.

He explained that this was the way to begin a positive friendly relationship that 'makes people feel special' and could then be built upon during the first year with regular invitations to observe lessons, share lunch, become involved with social events, join the Parent Teacher Association and perhaps become a school volunteer helping with reading and other classroom activities. He described this as being part of a team that could only benefit a child's learning and set the foundations for a strong relationship that would endure throughout their time at the school.

These are strategies that are well established in many schools, although these are non-statutory, and you might want to think about why home visits are sometimes controversial and might be problematic with respect to working with parents affected by living in poverty (Department for Education 2017).

Case study: Harvey

Harvey, aged 4, lives with his father, Ben, who is a lone parent, in bed and breakfast temporary accommodation in a multi-occupancy house. His mother lives in another part of the country and has minimal contact. Ben works afternoon and early evening shifts as an office cleaner and so Harvey is collected from his nursery by other family members who look after him at their various homes on weekdays until he is picked up and taken home at 7pm. They are travelling on public transport and do not usually arrive home until 8pm when it is time to prepare for bed.

How can Ben be made to feel valued at Harvey's future school?

There are clear benefits to working in partnership with all parents that include sustained involvement in the community served by the educational setting, reducing isolation and helping to build support networks. The ways in which partnership can be addressed is discussed with further examples in Chapter 6.

Conclusion

Working with parents, carers and the families of young children is never easy but always worthwhile. The particular circumstances of those affected by living in poverty need to be carefully considered in terms of preventing potential barriers to inclusive practice. However, well informed practitioners can create careful collaborative planning that ensures a productive partnership that will benefit all children's education.

Further Reading

Brooker, L. (2002) *Starting School – Young Children Learning Cultures.* Buckingham: Open University Press.

MacNaughton, G. and Hughes, P. (2011) *Parents and Professionals in Early Childhood Settings.* Maidenhead: Open University Press.

Useful websites

Pen Green Centre, www.pengreen.org

Thomas Coram Centre, www.thomascoram.camden.sch.uk

References

Brooker, L. (2002) *Starting School – Young Children Learning Cultures.* Buckingham: Open University Press.

Brotherton, G. and McGillivray, G. (2010) 'Changing Childhoods, Changing Families' in Brotherton, G., Davies, H. and McGillivray, G. (eds.) *Working with Children, Young People and Families.* London: Sage, pp. 16–32.

Central Advisory Council for Education (1967) *Children and their Primary Schools: A report of the Central Advisory Council for Education (England).* London: Department of Education and Science.

Crowley, M. and Wheeler, H. (2014) 'Working with parents in the Early Years' in Pugh, G. and Duffy, B. (eds.) *Contemporary Issues in the Early Years*, 6th Edition. London: Sage.

DCSF (2008) *The Early Years Foundation Stage: Setting the Standards for Learning, Development and Care for Children from Birth to Five.* Nottingham: DCSF Publications.

Department of Education (2012) 'Nutbrown Review: Foundations for Quality: The Independent Review of Early Education and Childcare Qualifications'. Available online at: https://www.gov.uk/government/uploads/system/uploads/attachment_data/file/175463/Nutbrown-Review.pdf (accessed: 31st July 2017).

Department for Education (2017) 'Home Visits in the EYFS'., Available online at: https://schoolleaders.thekeysupport.com/pupils-and-parents/engaging-parents-and-carers/building-relationships-with-parents/home-visits-eyfs/ (accessed: 18 May 2017).

DfE (2012) *Statutory Framework for the Early Years Foundation Stage 2012: Setting the Standards for Learning, Development and Care for Children from Birth to Five.* Runcorn: DfE Publications.

Moss, P. (13 March 2013) 'The Stories we tell about Early Childhood Education'. Lecture at Newman University (unpublished).

Mukherji, P. and Mummery, V. (2014) 'Working in partnership with parents in early childhood settings' in Mukherji, P. and Dryden, L. (eds.) *Foundations of Early Childhood*. London: Sage.

Odene, C. (2017) 'Can Parenting Be Taught?' Available online at: www.theguardian.com/lifeandstyle/2017/may/20/can-parenting-be-taught (accessed: 18 May 2017).

Parents Early Years and Learning (PEAL). Available online at: www.ncb.org.uk/what-we-do/our-priorities/early-years/projects-programmes/parents-early-years-learning (accessed: 18 May 2017).

Sharp, R., Green, A. and Lewis, J. (1975) *Education and Social Control: A Study in Progressive Education*. London: Routledge.

Sylva, K., Melhuish, E., Sammons, P., Siraj-Blatchford, I. & Taggart, B. (2004) *The Effective Provision of Pre-School Education (EPPE) Project: A Longitudinal Study funded by the DfES (1997–2003)*. Available online at: http://eppe.ioe.ac.uk/eppe/eppepdfs/bera1.pdf (accessed: 10 May 2017).

Tickell, C. (2011) *The Early Years: Foundations for life, health and learning – An Independent Report on the Early Years Foundation Stage to Her Majesty's Government*. Available online at: www.gov.uk/government/uploads/system/uploads/attachment_data/file/180919/DFE-00177-2011.pdf (accessed: 25 October 2016).

Whalley, M. and Dennison, M. (2007) 'Dialogue and Documentation: Sharing Information and Developing a Rich Curriculum' in M. Whalley and the Pen Green Team, *Involving Parents in their Children's Learning*. London: Paul Chapman Publishing.

Wrigley, T. (2012) 'Rethinking Poverty and Social Class: The Teacher's Response' in Arshad, R. Wrigley, T. and Pratt, L. (eds.) *Social Justice Re-examined*. London: Institute of Education Press.

Working in partnership

Karen Argent

With thanks to Engage Service, Solihull Council's Early Help Offer, for their assistance in the completion of this Chapter.

This chapter will explore the wide range of statutory and voluntary and community sector organisations which work in partnership with and offer some support to children, families and Early Years practitioners/settings. It includes the example of one Local Authority that uses a model of multi-agency family support work traditionally carried out in children's centres and other community organisations. It aims to help students/practitioners to understand the rapidly changing roles and dynamics of different professionals and sectors in the climate of shrinking public services, e.g. local libraries and Citizens Advice Centres.

It will also explore wider issues of inclusion and participation for children living in poverty within the local community and explore how working in partnership with all families requires some responsibility by individual practitioners to acquire a personal knowledge and understanding of the possible effects of poverty. The term 'multi-agency working' is often used to describe how different professionals within different sectors work together. A chapter in another book in this series *Disability and Inclusion in Early Years Education* (Collett 2017) has described this very well: "Taken at its most literal, the term 'agency', means simply 'action'; thus the agents in a child's life are the "actors", or those who act on his or her behalf." However, interpretation varies and Wall (2011: 18) suggests that there are a number of different ways in which professionals can work together, hence the subtle differences in terminology used.

- Collaborative working: professionals working together.

- Inter-agency/interdisciplinary: different professionals working in parallel, but in a more co-operative way.

- Multi-disciplinary/multi-professional/multi-agency working: a number of professionals working to support the child, but not necessarily together across professional boundaries – each providing their piece of the puzzle.

- Transagency/transdisciplinary: the implementation of a keyworker system with one professional taking responsibility for co-ordination, and regular meetings take place to share information, discuss progress and set joint goals.

It is interesting to note the emphasis on the role of expert professionals in these definitions. None include the individual service users in a community, i.e. children and their families, as playing a significant part in multi-agency working, even though they are assumed to be fully involved in decision making.

There has been much detail written elsewhere about the history of multi-agency working and the importance of what are often described as 'joined-up' approaches by Lumsdon (2014) and many other academic writers (e.g. Siraj-Blatchford et al. 2007; Gasper 2010), which I do not intend to repeat here. Collett (2017) provides a particularly clear overview of the different agencies involved in the care and education of young children. These remain a mix located in the statutory and non-statutory sectors made up of private, voluntary and community organisations. The role of the community sector has become increasingly important and can provide opportunities for providing services that are in tune with particular local community needs.

This means that Early Years practitioners can play a significant role in working in close formal partnership with agencies and develop more informal partnerships with the service users themselves. To achieve this includes developing an understanding of the benefits and challenges of working collaboratively and the skill of effective consultation with the children and their family members by not only listening to, but responding to their views. This might be uncomfortable and new territory for many professionals because of traditional views that can suggest that these service users are passive and powerless in a relationship with 'expert' Early Years providers.

What used to happen

The idea of Early Years practitioners working seamlessly in close partnership with a range of statutory and non-statutory organisations is certainly not a new one – *The Children Act* (DH 1989). However, one of the enduring difficulties in making this work well is the historical separation between childcare (mainly in the private and voluntary sector) and the parallel but differently funded Early Education provision (mainly in the statutory sector). Rather like the separation between health and social care in adult services, which have more in common than differences, the successful integration of education and childcare in order to provide effective 'Educare' continues to be elusive. Nobody would argue that working together for a common interest is desirable, but is it possible? With the best will in the world, differences in training, management structures, available resources, difficulties with communication and budget restrictions makes working together to effectively support the increasing number of children and families living in poverty a huge challenge. Taking care of the young children of the poorest has always been in the interests of society, if only to ensure that this enables their parents to work and for them to survive childhood in order to be able to be eventually employed in work themselves.

Penn (2005) provides a very good overview of the history of UK early childhood education and care, and discusses how ideas about provision can be traced back to the first workplace nursery provided by Robert Owen at his factory in New Lanark, Scotland, in 1818. He was a pioneer in trying to 'both protect children from the exploitation that accompanied the industrial revolution and the impact of poverty' (Pound 2014). However desirable, such provision was very unusual and the fate of most poor children under 5 for the rest of the nineteenth century was to be looked after within a very formal school system, one that certainly did not meet their holistic needs. Campaigning for more appropriate provision at the beginning of the twentieth century led to funding being withdrawn for children under 5 in schools in 1907. The consequent gap in provision eventually led to the formation of the Nursery Schools Association in 1923, led by Margaret and Rachel McMillan, who argued in a 1927 policy statement 'that nursery schools were places where children could be well looked after, unlike their cramped homes in cramped streets' (Penn 2005, p. 120). These sisters were leading activists who promoted the need for free school meals and the importance of regular school medicals to ensure that children would fully benefit from nursery education. A parallel twentieth-century movement was the National Society of Day Nurseries, which was founded to meet the needs of mothers who needed care for their children while they worked.

These were early examples of worthy initiatives to provide free good quality and safe 'joined up' childcare that addressed the holistic needs of young children and their working mothers. The evacuation of over 1 million children from urban areas to the countryside during World War II highlighted some very disadvantaged backgrounds, and the need for building much better housing and providing better overall care and education after the end of the war. However, emerging theories of child development by Bowlby emphasised the importance of mother–child attachment and directly challenged the desirability of young children being cared for outside the home (Pound 2014). Later, the influences of theorists like Piaget on the structure of schooling strongly influenced a major review of primary and nursery education. The Plowden Report (1967) stated:

'It's no large overall system which is needed … only in the last resort is there need to provide a substitute for those who are completely unable to manage themselves …'

(quoted in Penn 2005, p. 123).

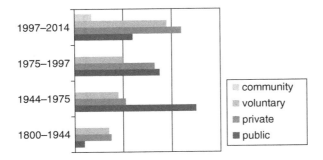

Figure 6.1 Changing dynamics of the different sectors (Collett 2017).

Alongside emerging economic constraints this meant that nursery pro-vision soon changed from being an entitlement to all round full-time care and education. Inadequate statutory provision led to the formation of the Pre-school Playgroup Association (now the Pre-School Learning Alliance) in 1962, a community-led voluntary association staffed by mostly middle-class mothers as volunteers. Early Years services in the UK evolved into a mostly part-time complicated patchwork of statutory, pri-vate and voluntary early provision post World War II to the present day.

It is clear that the role of the different sectors was changing due to many influences and that the proportion of agencies located in the statutory sector reached its peak in the 30 years after the end of World War II as a direct result of the introduction of the Welfare State in 1948.

More recent developments

In 1998, a new Labour government placed a clear emphasis on the need for better joined up working through community-based Sure Start Local programmes, early excellence centres and neighbourhood nurs-eries all of which were inspired by a US project called 'HeadStart', and seemed to promise that an economic investment in good quality Early Years provision would eventually have a tangible impact on growing a healthy and wealthy society. The idea was that well-resourced and

easily accessible provision for all children under 5 staffed by well-qual-
ified professionals would help to create positive attitudes and enthusi-
asm for learning.

Soon after, came the Every Child Matters (ECM) framework (2004), an
overarching policy which emerged from evident failings in multi-agency
working, exposed as a result of the serious case review into the death
of Victoria Climbie in 2000. Some of you will remember the 'Five Outcomes', which framed good practice in all children's services across the
sectors at the time. One of these that focussed on addressing children
living in poverty was 'Achieving Economic Wellbeing', which was probably the most difficult to translate into practice. The Childcare Act (2006)
placed legal responsibilities on local authorities to improve integrated
under-fives provision. Part of the ECM agenda was the Common Assessment Framework (CAF), which was used if there were concerns about
a child and required a lead practitioner to co-ordinate the most helpful
form of intervention in collaboration with family and other agencies.

Terminology soon changed again to give us the idea of 'the team
around the child' – all different manifestations of the same set of ideas
i.e., it is a good idea to work collaboratively in partnership with the
family for the sake of the child.

In 2010, the new Coalition government continued to recognise the
significance of offering Early Years services, and free nursery education
for 2-year-olds in disadvantaged areas was introduced in 2010 as a further incentive to working parents. However, the ring fencing of funding
for children's centres and other Early Years centres was removed with
some detrimental impact (see Uren in Pugh & Duffy 2014).

The emphasis shifted towards placing more onus on individual parents to be able to make even more choices for their children. This had
a particular impact on children with special educational needs and
disabilities (see Collett 2017).

Bringing things up to date

The Coalition government (2010–15) led by David Cameron promoted the idea of everyone belonging to 'The Big Society', with an

increased role for the voluntary sector in filling the gaps in provision. Whilst this was something that had been going on for a long time in local communities, the emphasis here was largely about the economic benefits of not relying on expensive statutory services. The phrase 'we are all in it together' was coined to give further weight to the idea that society needed to be careful and cautious about funding. This government message was that many public services were wasteful and required streamlining, modernising and reorganisation, often shifting responsibility to the private sector, which would be more 'efficient'.

In practical terms, this was translated into overseeing financial cuts to local authorities with the resulting pressure on how they would manage a severely reduced budget but still deliver a range of effective services. Difficult decisions were made by individual authorities to prioritise where money was most needed and to reshape or cut those services that were not seen as essential. Withdrawal of funding for Citizens Advice Bureaux and local libraries was a good example of this because these were controversially no longer viewed as 'essential' services in competition with, for example, funding elderly social care. Consequently, existing services have often been merged and located on the same site to save money on buildings, staff and other resources.

This competition for funding continues to be problematic for Early Years provision, particularly because of diminished budgets for children's centres and other family support services. Nursery schools in the statutory sector are also struggling to survive due to changes in funding. This puts further pressure onto access to nursery classes in schools and ultimately reduces choices for parents and their children. Increasingly, the role of Sure Start has been transformed and shifted to focus on providing parenting advice and preparing children to start school rather than providing the wide range of services and opportunities for partnership with families that characterised it as an innovative, but very expensive model.

The Conservative government (2016–17) led by Theresa May has recently shifted the responsibility for a 'joined up' approach still further with the slogan of 'a shared society' that moves the focus away from meeting the needs of those living in poverty towards families that are struggling to make ends meet:

> You have a job but no job security; you just about manage but worry about the cost of living and getting your children into a good school; you put in long hours – working to live and living to work – but your wages have stagnated and there is little left over at the end of the month.
>
> (Charity Commission 2017)

Reflective activity

Kelly is an unemployed lone parent who claims Jobseekers Allowance. Her 5-year-old son Callum draws a picture about his weekend on Monday morning at school, which shows everyone wearing coats in the cold house. He explains that there was nothing to eat apart from cornflakes.

What could you do to help?

Access to statutory benefits such as Jobseekers Allowance is increasingly complex and conditional, in other words, if a claimant fails to strictly comply with the various rules, this can result in benefits being completely cut. For instance, being allowed to claim Jobseekers Allowance now requires evidence of a fixed number of hours being spent actively looking for work. This evidence is required to be presented regularly and by appointment at the local job centre. If this is deemed insufficient, benefits can be suspended, which is what has happened in this case as Kelly had not been able to provide evidence of face-to-face conversations she had with several prospective employers as she trailed round local shops looking for work. A similar sanction can be applied if an individual misses or is late for an appointment at the job centre and this can be particularly difficult if it happens on a Friday or prior to a public holiday. Circumstances can now arise where individual benefits can be sanctioned for up to three months – in other words, no access to any money at all without going through a complex bureaucratic process to request emergency funding in the form of a loan that has to later be deducted from subsequent benefits. Lack of access to adequate financial support in a crisis like this can mean that some families are in danger of relying on loan companies that demand high interest and other conditions. The Child Poverty Action Group (CPAG) is one of many anti-poverty campaigning organisations and explains that there has been an escalation of benefit sanctions since 2010, which have come to play a major role in contributing to extreme poverty. Concerns about the effectiveness of such sanctions led to the Oakley Review, which was commissioned under the terms of the Job-seekers (Back to Work Schemes) Act 2013 and includes a broad range of evidence from relevant organisations and individuals.

Kelly would certainly benefit from access to emergency advice as soon as the problem arises, and many schools and other Early Years set-tings can be the hub for support and advice. I have been fortunate to experience some very good multi-agency partnership during my work-ing life, although it wasn't called that at the time. For instance, my first teaching post in 1980 was in a special school and there I was impressed at the well-established and ongoing dialogue between education, health and social services professionals who were concerned to work alongside families for the benefit of the child. Special schools continue to be mod-els of effective partnership working – they work very closely with fami-lies recognising that they often have specialist knowledge of their child's condition that needs to be shared with everyone concerned. Working in a special school also highlighted for me the importance of the voluntary sector in providing advice from organisations like Shelter and specialist disability charities like Mencap that had been emerging at that time.

Beyond the very good multi-agency working in special schools in the 1980s and 1990s, there seemed to be varying degrees of co-operation between the different professions and sectors. However, working in a nursery school in a poor inner-city area made me aware of voluntary organisations like the Birmingham Settlement, which continues to pro-vide a valuable community hub for training, support and advice for peo-ple struggling with housing problems, unemployment and debt and also provided access to training and employment. Although I came across these good examples, working in the education sector sheltered me from the real world of multi-agency working. I left teaching in 2000 to become an inclusion worker, working in the community with families of children with disabilities, employed by the charity KIDS as part of the first Sure Start programme in Birmingham. This new initiative meant working closely alongside health visitors, social workers and a range of other Early Years professionals and really opened my eyes to what I had been missing.

Reflective activity

- How would you describe your own background?

- Which voluntary organisations that help people living in poverty do you already know about?

- Do you work in partnership with any agencies from different sectors?

- What would you do to provide advice and support for Kelly?

- Where would you go for advice?

Personal perspectives

Perceptions of practitioners about poverty and social exclusion and how these can be addressed are partly shaped by individual personal experiences. Since people working in the Early Years sector are not particularly well paid, many will have relevant circumstances as a result of financial hardship and related difficulties. Whether or not this helps to develop an empathetic response is debatable but it is important for all practitioners, whatever their background and experiences to recognise but to be objective about personal perspectives. Others may come from a background where a certain standard of living is taken for granted and believe that anyone who does not conform to this template is lacking in some way. You may not always agree with how some parents appear to spend a limited income but as a professional, it is important to be able to stand back and be non-judgemental. Only in this way can a respectful partnership be achieved.

Wrigley (2012, p. 155) has pointed out how individual attitudes to poverty are shaped from an early age so that those working with children need to recognise these influences on their professional practice. He explains that many teachers are frustrated by what they perceive as a lack of interest and engagement by many parents rather than thinking about why they might find it difficult to work in partnership with a school. For instance, not turning up to discuss their child's progress for a parents' evening could be for many reasons 'including irregular working hours, the need to look after other children or feelings of anxiety or antipathy towards school – a legacy of their own negative experiences of schooling'.

In the same way, individuals will have differing attitudes to working in partnership and which agencies do what, why and when. Like many people, I grew up in a lower middle-class family with a reasonable standard of living. I think that my perception of poverty and who might be able to help individuals was a common one. It was largely based on what I saw in the media about charitable organisations like the Salvation Army and I was aware that they worked throughout the year, not just at Christmas, to provide support for destitute people. Moving away from home in the 1970s, I learnt the difficulties of managing to live on a student grant in not very nice rented accommodation. I decided to make contact with local council officials and housing associations for advice – fortunately, I knew where to go and what to ask when I got there because I was reasonably confident, articulate and un-intimidated by authority. In the 1980s, I gained a more nuanced perspective about what it meant to live in poverty from friends who worked in the front line of social services who told me about visiting people living in far worse circumstances, and how the benefits system was designed to provide temporary but often inadequate financial support. Later I also had some personal experiences of being a lone parent on a limited income and some family experiences of the effects of unemployment. But I was always cushioned against the extreme consequences of poverty by my relatively rich social and cultural capital. This meant that I could always rely on the help and support from informal networks of family and friends if needed.

This is not necessarily the case for families who may be struggling to live on a very limited income in a community where many others may be in similar circumstances. Managing to live on a very limited income in poor housing has always been problematic but since the foundation of the Welfare State in 1948, the difficulties of living in poverty has been recognised as being the responsibility of everyone in society. This has meant that the government provides some financial support for those who qualify for help in the form of a range of benefits. However, relying on these as a source of income to maintain a decent standard of living is certainly not the easy life that is sometimes portrayed in some sections of the media.

Some positive strategies

Despite an increasingly draconian policy context, it is important to remain optimistic about working in partnership because there are many examples of positive strategies for the challenge of working with limited services, continuing to innovate and collaborate effectively to meet the needs of vulnerable children and their families. Early Years practitioners can continue to work with families and to sensitively signpost them to services outside the setting if appropriate.

Solihull, a Local Authority case study

Selena comes from a middle-class family with parents in full-time employment, both working as health professionals in the local hospital. She has a Level 3 Childcare qualification and is in the first year of studying for a part time Foundation Degree in Early Years. Since qualifying, she has worked for 3 years in several other nursery settings with young children, mostly in the private sector. She now works as a teaching assistant in a reception class at Golden Field Primary School with 28 children, aged between 4 and 5. It is located in an area with a majority of social housing, privately rented and some owner-occupied houses. There is high unemployment and most working parents have part-time, minimum-wage jobs.

Before working at this school, she did not realise how many ordinary people struggled to provide a decent standard of living for their children in very difficult circumstances. This awareness and the development of empathy is a necessary first step in providing sensitive family support that will benefit everyone concerned. She works alongside an experienced teacher and is also fortunate to be employed at a school in Solihull, West Midlands, which is a Local Authority that is keen to promote good 'joined up' Early Years provision (Solihull Partnership 2014). The school is planning an educational visit to a local farm and three of the children in the class are giving Selena particular concern:

Case study: Three 4-year-old children in a reception class

Poppy lives in hostel temporary accommodation with her unemployed mother and brother, aged 6, who attends the same school. Dad has recently started a 2-year prison sentence for offences related to domestic violence. She is a very quiet child who has difficulty mixing with her peers. She often appears to be tired and listless.

Mother is reluctant to talk with staff and rarely comes to assemblies etc. She is often late collecting her children due to appointments and other commitments.

Omar is a recently arrived Syrian refugee, living in private rented accommodation with his father who is seeking to work as a car mechanic, pregnant mother and sister aged 6. He is finding it difficult to separate from mother at the start of the school day. He is slowly beginning to settle into the school routine but lacks concentration. He sometimes lashes out at other children. Both parents are very keen to become involved with the school but finding it difficult to communicate with other parents and to feel part of the community.

Jasmine lives in a Housing Association maisonette with her mother, who works part time as a cleaner, dad who works part time as a shift worker in social care and twin sisters aged 2, one of whom has cerebral palsy. She is a very emotional child who cries a lot and clings to staff rather than playing with her peers. Both parents are very concerned about her progress and often come to talk to staff about this.

Selena works in Solihull, in the West Midlands, which is an example of a Local Authority that may be perceived from the outside as being relatively affluent. But like many such places in England it also has more average and mixed communities, including some pockets of deprivation. It has been chosen as a case study for this chapter because, despite the many funding and organisational challenges faced by all local authorities, it continues to successfully support families through innovative multi-agency working. The Solihull Healthy Child Programme (0–19 Years) (Solihull Partnership 2015a), with guidance from Public Health England, stresses the need for 'integrated pathways' to enable fast access to specialist services and emphasises the need for all parts of Early Help services to work together. As part of this, the Service Specification 2017–20 makes reference to significant World Health Organisation research 2007, and points out that 'successive academic and economic reviews have demonstrated the economic and social value of prevention and early intervention programmes in pregnancy and the 0–19 years. In fact, the evidence base for improved health, social and educational outcomes from a systematic approach to early childhood development has never been stronger and has been described as a powerful equalizer which merits investment'.

Early Help 0–19 services have recently been reorganised and although there are no longer any children's centres located in physical buildings, the authority has a longstanding commitment to provide a children's centre and offer 0–19 services in an integrated manner and so is able to offer community venues for services to achieve this.

Available services include:

- Information and advice to parents and prospective parents.

- Collaborative Action Groups that help to inform the Local Authority (LA) assessments re strengths and needs across an area.

- Community modules that provide self-confidence training to assist parents or prospective parents.

The specific needs of families living in poverty are now recognised and centrally supported via a range of initiatives.

These include information and access to advice from services such as the Family Nurse partnership and the Mental Health Team. The Family Nurse partnership is available to all first-time mums who are under 19 and pregnant with their first child. The Solihull 'Early Help' team aims to offer support at the earliest opportunity via what is known as 'Solihull Engage'. This service tries hard to reach service users in a variety of different ways such as providing Family Support Workers (FSW). They can offer a range of advice including signposting to information re accessing benefits and support for debt management. They can also provide more targeted work to wrap around existing early intervention strategies, for example, if a family requires help with a particular parenting issue which has been picked up by the health visitor or the school. 'Solihull Engage' uses a variety of communication methods:

- A range of social media including a website, Facebook page, twitter account and Instagram.

- Working with partners to facilitate half termly community hubs, which provide support and information to children, young people and families.

- A key worker is allocated to one or two schools. This role is to improve communication across the school and to share key messages.

- Collaborative Action Groups – a termly forum.

So, there is plenty of support within this Local Authority for Selena to tap into if she wants to find out more. However, she needs to be proactive in the following ways:

- Find out more about how the school is already involved with the Solihull Local Authority initiative Early Help strategy that promotes and supports joined up working.

- Understand that Early Help is everyone's business and that she can play her part.

- Ask whether she can undertake the Early Help one-day training.

- Find out about other relevant multi-disciplinary training. For example, Solihull promotes 'solution focussed' approaches and now includes Mental Health First Aid training, which is available as a result of the recent government initiative to improve awareness and intervention.

- Find out about how the authority uses 'Signs of Safety', a reputable constructive child-centred approach used to identify and prevent safeguarding issues.

Early Help

Every Local Authority has developed different responses to the need for professionals to work in better partnership. Some still retain an adapted version of the Common Assessment Framework (CAF) that was part of ECM until the different approach required by the Coalition government of 2010. Others, like Solihull have evolved a bespoke strategy that is made available through regular training sessions for those working in different sectors. Like CAF, this approach relies on the voluntary engagement of children and their families. A request for support can be made by the school, family or health services, but always with the consent of the family concerned. This is based around five core principles:

Box 6.1 The Five Core Principles of Early Help

1. Causes not symptoms

Sustainable positive change for individuals depends on tackling the causes of problems rather than constantly seeking to deal with the presenting symptoms. This reinforces a culture of independence.

2. Lives not services

Early Help organisations are made up of staff who practice Early Help. This means focusing on quality of relationships

---

with and quality of life for families, not just managing risk and reducing harm. It means constructive team working between the organisations, communities and families, providing personalised, integrated and caring support, and making every relationship count.

3. Families and communities can deliver *earlier* help

Early Help has the best chance of success where individuals and their families feel supported to find their own solutions to the issues facing them. This help often comes from within the family or community, and much earlier than help from statutory services. Families and communities are also better at finding personalised low-cost solutions which are easier to sustain over time.

4. Early childhood help

Help in the first 3 years of life is an investment that pays back for a lifetime, and offers a chance to break intergeneration cycles of poor outcomes.

5. Not all help is equal

The measure of Early Help is the outcome, not the effort, and some interventions have more impact than others. This means investing in programmes which have an evidence base, or building an evidence base where none exists. It also means fidelity, applying evidence-based programmes in the way that they have been designed and evaluated.

(Adapted from 'Early Help' training materials, Solihull Local Authority)

If a concern is expressed, a trusted person will be recognised, which will be either the original requester of or the FSW, who will co-ordinate one of several ways forward ranging from low-key ongoing intervention, which can include signposting to relevant information, through to levels of more targeted support that is decided as a result of a multi-agency 'team around the family' meeting resulting in an agreed action plan. The principles of Early Support are then applied by 'Engage', which ensures that coherent joined up practice takes place. See Figure 6.2.

If Selena was able to undertake the one-day Module One Early Help training she would have a much better understanding of the principles of Early Help and both their role and the role of Engage within it. The training also supports practitioners to complete the engagement tool, a vital part of the request for help process. This means that Selena, in collaboration with her other school colleagues, would be able to improve their understanding and confidence when working effectively in the long term with the families of the three children.

The farm visit

Selena's immediate challenge is to ensure that all three children are able to come on and to enjoy the educational trip to the farm. Schools now have a variety of charging policies for funding trips and other additional activities. Some will request a one-off 'voluntary contribution' from every parent and expect this to be paid in advance. Others will ask for a regular payment to be made to cover the costs and this

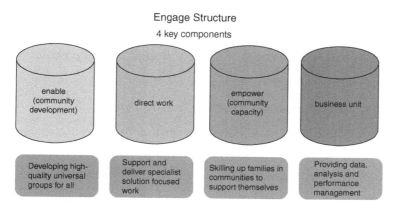

Figure 6.2 The Engage structure of Solihull Local Authority.

can be spread throughout the school year. Others may choose to raise funds for these activities via events such as jumble sales and sponsored events.

If 'voluntary contributions' from parents are required, then it is very important that no undue pressure is put onto parents who may struggle to find the amount, however small, otherwise they may be tempted to withdraw their child from the trip as a consequence. Hopefully, discussions and guidance about charging for trips takes place with all the staff and also there are contingency plans if a child's parents do not make a contribution for the visit. No child should be excluded from going on the school trip, whether their parent has paid or not, as this is part of their educational entitlement. Just imagine how a child would feel if they arrived to find that they were not permitted to go to the farm with all their friends because the school insisted on payment. The initial cost is not the only potential problem for some families to meet. Children who are entitled to free school dinners would be provided with a free packed lunch but there may also be costs associated with going on the trip, for instance relevant clothes, wellington boots and spending money, which could also be very difficult. In partnership with senior members of school staff, the following overall points could be addressed at the beginning of every school year to anticipate and avoid organisational problems:

- What is the school's charging policy?
- Are the needs of families with a restricted income sufficiently addressed?
- Are all school staff aware of the need for sensitivity?
- What are the expectations regarding suitable clothing?
- How can these be addressed without stigmatising individual children?
- Are there ways to ensure that all children and all families feel included in the preparation and follow up work from the visit?
- Are there cultural sensitivities about the child going on a school trip?

What might long-term partnership look like in practice?

Due to their circumstances, Engage may already be involved with Omar, Poppy and Jasmine, who are causing Selena concerns. Engage could support by recommending a free parenting course to help them to understand and then constructively manage a child's behaviour. The 'Understanding your child's behaviour' course offered in this LA emphasises the importance of building strong attachment between parents/carers and their children, and embedding the idea of reciprocity in fostering respectful interactions. As some parents are unable or unwilling to participate in a physical group, an online course will shortly be made available so that everyone can access it according to individual need and preference.

Each of the three children has complicated but by no means untypical backgrounds that will contribute to their difficult circumstances. Everyone is unique but some factors affecting them are increasingly commonplace in many Early Years settings throughout the UK, for example, the effects of poor housing, domestic violence, newly arrived status, low income and unemployment. There are plenty of practical ways in which they and their families can be offered further support and, therefore, be helped to feel included in the school community.

Working in partnership with Poppy's family

This family is living in temporary hostel accommodation, which is far from ideal as it is probably cramped and lacking in privacy. The school can play its part by giving the message to mum that the family's welfare is a priority and that they will be supportive in trying to move somewhere more permanent. This might include liaising with housing support personnel and helping her to attend appointments at more convenient times.

With her permission (and on a need-to-know basis), it is important that relevant school staff are aware of the circumstances and to be mindful of potential impact on sleep and limited opportunities for play and a quiet place to complete homework activities. The school FSW may discuss with mum about how to manage bedtime routines in these difficult circumstances. Attending a universal parenting class could be helpful or one that more specifically builds confidence.

Staff may need some training about the effects of family imprisonment, including the stresses of separation, keeping in touch and prison visits, if this happens. There are many support organisations, e.g. i-HOP that can provide information and advice for those affected and different professionals (see Chapter 7 for examples of this). Access to the internet via school may be very helpful in this respect as it is unlikely that mum will have easy access at the hostel.

Staff may need some training about the effects of domestic violence. The family support worker can help with ensuring access to domestic violence support organisations, although this is probably already underway as a result of the father's conviction.

As with all parents, the staff can think about how mum can better access formal and informal networks at the school. This means finding time to talk with her about how she might get more involved. It is important to be sensitive about this approach as she has a lot of difficulties that need to be resolved. However, she may feel encouraged if invited to participate in some way. Perhaps she would like to come along on the trip to the farm as a welcome distraction for a few hours. An inclusive setting facilitates getting to know all its parents, including knowing about any particular interests and hobbies that they might feel happy to contribute to the life of school community. This can range from helping with school trips, having expertise in a subject like collecting stamps or making toys, or perhaps growing plants or baking to help with fund raising events.

Working in partnership with Omar's family

It is important for individual practitioners to have some overall background knowledge and understanding about the effect of war and displacement in relation to asylum seekers and refugees, particularly in relation to children. How to do this will be further explored in Chapter 7, but some preparatory training for staff is essential in order to ensure that

Omar and his family feel welcome in the school. Solihull is one of the local authorities that is participating in the fully funded Syrian Vulnerable Person Resettlement scheme that guarantees a safe place and a new home for a small number of Syrian families from refugee camps. To support this, there is a member of the Engage team who co-ordinates provision for these families as soon as they arrive in England as responsibility then passes from the Home Office to a Local Authority, which then provides ongoing information and family support. There is considerable preparatory liaison work, which will have taken place before Omar and his family arrive. Part of the remit is to make effective links with local schools and work in partnership with other organisations to raise awareness about the scheme and to provide information about the particular needs of a family that is coming to make a new home in the area.

Preparatory liaison includes:

- Home office.
- Benefits.
- Housing.
- Interpreters.
- Schools admissions.
- Schools.
- Pre-school.
- SEND.
- Landlords.
- Voluntary coordinator.
- Befriending service.
- Health e.g. GP and dentist, psychological support, e.g. counselling.
- ESOL/ College liaison.
- Link to faith groups.

'Engage' family support

- Preparation of home.
- Meeting the family.
- Supporting individual children including preparation for school/pre-school.
- Facilitating ESOL classes.
- Arranging council financial support, e.g. for school uniforms etc.

Working in partnership with Jasmine's family

The complex work patterns of Jasmine's parents are not unusual as many people juggle more than one part-time job and still have great difficulty in making ends meet. This means that the school staff may need to be flexible as to when they are available to meet with such parents. The 2-year-old with cerebral palsy (CP) will already be identified as benefitting from support from the SEND team and it is important to liaise with them with permission from the parents. It is also important to know the extent to which the health visitor is involved as the parents may need help with completing the education and health assessment. This will ensure that the twin with CP is receiving any necessary specialist support like physiotherapy and speech and language therapy if necessary. The FSW could facilitate this dialogue through requesting a 'team around the family' meeting to ensure that the whole family is getting the necessary advice and support. For instance, it may be that Jasmine is worrying about her twin siblings for different reasons. The Engage worker could contribute by discussing the concerns about Jasmine's anxiety and offer a parenting class if this would be helpful.

Siblings of children with SEND can often feel the effects of worrying about all kinds of related issues. They can also feel that their parent's attention is focussed on this sibling and that they are not as important. There are all kinds of voluntary organisations that offer fun activities and advice for parents for this very reason, which could be signposted by the FSW.

Staff may benefit from training about the demands of shift work and complex work patterns in order to be creative about involving this family fully in the life of the school. It may be difficult for either parent to come to help on the school trip to the farm but they might be interested in helping with some follow-up activities at home.

Effective and respectful partnership working by knowledgeable practitioners focuses on signposting all family members towards additional resources as well as being able to develop their confidence and independence, and emphasising what they can contribute to the partnership that will ultimately benefit their child's experience of education.

What does Selena need to think about before discussing her concerns about each of these children with other school staff? How can she go about working in partnership with the families and other agencies? Can you think about any potential barriers? How can these be addressed in a professional manner?

Implications for the school setting

Selena is a teaching assistant, an important professional role that means she will have lots of direct daily contact with family members that drop off and collect their children. She will play a key part in developing positive relationships and possibly communicate regularly in an informal way with parents and carers more frequently than other school staff. It needs to be pointed out that, however important this role is, she occupies a relatively lowly place in the school hierarchy in terms of influence. All members of staff contribute to the ethos of a school but decisions about how to ensure that a school is an effective, inclusive learning environment for those living in poverty may need much further discussion and endorsement at a senior management level. Once this has hopefully happened it is important to think about how to best communicate all the relevant information to parents, families, practitioners and other professionals.

This may include implications for ongoing staff training and a review of all school policies and procedures. For instance, facilities might be put in place to ensure that the school is a community hub of support for subjects that could affect many families at different times whilst their children attend the school. These might include providing information about:

- Funding school trips and other events.

- Breakfast and after school clubs.

- Providing homework facilities for children who have nowhere suitable at home.

- Debt counselling.

- Access to council documents and talks to be made available for all parents on subjects that may be of concern relating to managing a limited budget, for example issues relating to fuel poverty (Solihull Partnership 2015b).

A very useful practical development is an online directory of available services across the Local Authority which is managed by Solihull family information service. This resource can be accessed at any time by practitioners and service users. Solihull Local Authority has developed further incentives for organisations to improve their practice in relation to partnership working. They have already developed a community champion's award to ensure that high quality services are commended and recognised. So, once a school (or a voluntary organisation) has provided evidence and therefore achieved the award, a symbol will be placed next to their name on the directory. There are three levels: Bronze denotes a safe organisation; Silver denotes that an organisation has all the correct and necessary procedures and processes in place; and Gold demonstrates that it has succeeded in empowering and supporting others. Volunteering pathways have also been developed that provide structured ways in which people can volunteer and access opportunities.

Conclusion

This chapter has provided some historical background about the considerable benefits for the wellbeing of children of working in partnership with different agencies, including parents and families. Doing this well has had several manifestations and the way it is interpreted depends to a large extent on the government in power at any time. The post-war consensus meant that most people agreed with the development of a generous and humane welfare system that cared for everyone 'from cradle to grave', and recognised the need for this to be funded through taxation. The recent drift towards a target driven, more conditional approach to welfare, as explained in Chapter 2 means that government now provides relatively limited resources to fund appropriate support for working in partnership. Despite this, local authorities may respond to this positively by ensuring that early intervention initiatives flourish and become more streamlined in order to avoid the potential waste of overlapping of services and ensure the benefits of working in more efficient partnership. Working effectively across different sectors has always been very challenging because it relies on excellent communication, time, well-trained practitioners and many other resources. However, doing this has clear advantages for children and their families in terms of actively reducing the many negative effects of living in poverty. This can be achieved by providing access to information, education and relevant support relating to the effects of poor housing, meeting physical and mental health needs and many other issues.

Many people are fortunate in being able to navigate a way through the occasional difficulties that life throws up because they have well-established, rich social and cultural capital acquired from an early age. This means that they have the advantage of being relatively confident in knowing how to access information and relevant people to help sort out a range of problems. On the other hand, the effects of poverty are multiple and personal circumstances are unpredictable for everyone, myself included. For example, I'm not sure that I would know where to turn if someone in my family was arrested and imprisoned and, as a consequence, I was unable to keep up with my mortgage repayments. A caring society looks after people in such situations and recognises their need for advice and practical support.

Working with families who are struggling to manage to bring up their children due to many circumstances relating to poverty and other circumstances can sometimes feel very frustrating. However, it can also mean working in close partnership with them and other support agencies to help build confidence and independence. In the process of doing this work with individuals, it is possible to develop very useful resources that benefit a whole community, particularly when this is based in a local school – a familiar friendly location that is easy to access. As already described, the example of the Solihull Early Help strategy focuses on early intervention and prevention and not just on managing risk and reducing harm. Families, children and young people are at the centre of all their work and this includes the development of good quality relationships and enhancing the outcomes for families. It means constructive team working between the organisations, communities and families, providing personalised, integrated and caring support, and making every 'relationship count'.

Acknowledging the need for developing knowledge and understanding the needs of others is an important part of being a reflective and empathetic member of a community. Undertaking relevant training and taking personal responsibility for finding out about accessing local services and support is also a mark of becoming an inclusive Early Year's practitioner.

Further reading

Hood, A. & Johnson, P. (2016) 'Are We "All in this Together?"' Available online at: https://www.ifs.org.uk/publications/8210 (accessed: 15 May 2017).

Mukeherji, P. & Dryden, L. (eds.) (2014) *Foundations of Early Childhood*. London: Sage.

References

Birmingham Settlement. Available online at: www.birminghamsettlement.org.uk/ (accessed: 15 May 2017).

Collett, C. (ed.) (2017) *Disability and Inclusion in Early Years Education*. London: Routledge.

CPAG 'Oakley Review'. Available online at: www.cpag.org.uk/content/sanctions (accessed: 7 February 2017).

Debt Counselling Solihull. Available online at: http://solihull.debt-management-site.com/debt-counselling.php (accessed: 15 May 2017).

DfES (2004) *Every Child Matters: Change for Children*. Department for Education and Skills. London: HMSO.

DH (1989) *The Children Act*. London: HMSO.

'Engage'. Available online at: http://engage@solihull.gov.uk (accessed: 15 May 2017).

Family Information Service Directory. Available online at: http://socialsolihull.org.uk/localoffer/family-information-service-directory/ (accessed: 15 May 2017).

Gasper, M. (2010) *Multi-Agency Working in the Early Years*. London: Sage.

'Guidance to support the commissioning of The Healthy Child Programme 0–19: health visiting and school nurse services (commissioning Guide 1)'. Available online at: www.gov.uk/government/publications/healthy-child-programme-0-to-19-health-visitor-and-school-nurse-commissioning (accessed: 15 May 2017).

Joseph Rowntree Trust (2016) 'In Work Poverty Reaches Record High as the Housing Crisis Fuels Insecurity'. Available online at: www.jrf.org.uk/press/work-poverty-hits-record-high-housing-crisis-fuels-insecurity (accessed: 15 May 2017).

Lumsden, E. 'Joined-up Thinking in Practice: An Exploration of Professional Collaboration' in Waller, T. and Davis, G. (eds.) (2014) *An Introduction to Early Childhood* (3rd edition), London: Sage.

May, T. (2017) 'The shared society: Prime Minister's speech at the Charity Commission annual meeting'. Available online at: www.gov.uk/government/speeches/the-shared-society-prime-ministers-speech-at-the-charity-commission-annual-meeting (accessed: 5 May 2017).

Penn, H. (2005) *Understanding Early Childhood: Issues and Controversies*. Maidenhead: Open University Press.

Pound, Linda (2014) 'The Historical Background of Early Childhood Care and education' in *Signs of Safety in England*. Available online at: www.nspcc.org.uk/services-and-resources/research-and-resources/2013/signs-of-safety-model-england/ (accessed 15 May 2017).

Siraj-Blatchford, I., Clarke, K. & Needham, M. (eds.) (2007) *The Team around the Child: Multi-Agency Working in the Early Years*. Stoke-on-Trent: Trentham Books.

Solihull Partnership (2014) 'Solihull's Early Help Strategy 2014–16'. Available online at: www.solihull.gov.uk/Portals/0/Partnership/SolihullEarlyHelpStrategy.pdf (accessed: 15 May 2017).

Solihull Partnership (2015a) Healthy Child Programme (0–19 years) in Solihull. Available online at: www.solihull.gov.uk/Portals/0/Consultations/Solihull_Vision_and_Pathway.pdf (accessed: 6 May 2017).

Solihull Partnership (2015b) 'Home energy efficiency and affordable warmth strategy: Keeping out the cold' (2015). Available online at: www.solihull.gov.uk/Portals/0/StrategiesPlansPolicies/Housing/EnergyandAffordable-WarmthStrategy.pdf (accessed: 15 May 2017).

'Syrian Resettlement Fact Sheet'. Available online at: www.gov.uk/government/uploads/system/uploads/attachment_data/file/472020/SyrianResettlement_Fact_Sheet_gov_uk.pdf (accessed: 15 May 2017).

The Stationery Office 'Childcare Act 2006'. Available online at: www.legislation.gov.uk/ukpga/2006/21/pdfs/ukpga_20060021_en.pdf (accessed: 15 May 2017).

Uren, L. (2014) 'Facing Austerity: the Local Authority Response' in Pugh, G. and Duffy, B. (eds.) *Contemporary Issues in the Early Years*. London: Sage.

Wall, K. (2011) *Special Needs and Early Years*, London: Sage.

Wrigley, T. (2012) 'Rethinking poverty and social class: The teacher's response' in Arshad, R.,Wrigley, T. and Pratt, L. (eds.) *Social Justice Re-examined: Dilemmas and Solutions for the Classroom Teacher*. Stoke on Trent: Trentham Books Ltd.

Resources

Karen Argent

This chapter will discuss the ways in which Early Years practitioners can increase their own knowledge and understanding of child poverty and avoid adopting a deficit model with reference to information and resources from well-established campaigning organisations like 'Shelter' and 'End Child Poverty'. It will also explore some teaching resources used with children that reflect a wide range of living circumstances. These can include picture books, which can be used as a starting point for raising awareness of diverse communities. Evidence suggests that attitudes to difference are shaped from a very early age and that all children respond well to positive images that represent a range of individuals and communities. Providing such powerful resources as part of an inclusive learning environment is clearly endorsed in the revised statutory framework for the Early Years Foundation Stage (Department for Education (DfE) 2017, p.12), which emphasises the need for children 'to know that other children don't always enjoy the same things, and are sensitive to this. They know about similarities and differences between themselves and others, and among families, communities and traditions'. It will include some examples of picture books that can be used to specifically and positively represent the particular characteristics of children living in a range of family environments as a 'normal' part of the social landscape. The chapter will also emphasise the ways in which a setting can provide opportunities to access a range of toys and activities that might not be available at home.

In Chapter 6, I discussed how attitudes to people living in poverty are shaped by a number of complex factors such as personal experiences alongside wider societal influences including the mainstream media. Being able to acknowledge these, often negative, perceptions is the first stage in growing to be an inclusive practitioner.

In Chapter 2, it was pointed out that it is essential for an inclusive practitioner to be aware of, and guard against, negative rhetoric that can be directed at children and families on the basis of their socio-economic status, which may in turn be a consequence of a number of factors, such as employment circumstances, family dynamics or where and how a child and family live. As with all good Early Years practice, this means that practitioners need to have a good understanding of children's home experiences to make sure that their activities and learning opportunities are presented in a relevant way by using points of reference that children can easily relate to. This means developing meaningful effective partnerships with parents so that individual children's interests and family culture can be embraced and valued. It is important to be aware that children's 'cultural capital' may take varying forms that can be exploited to enhance learning. In this way, Early Years settings and the practitioners that work in them can be very powerful in either reinforcing negative dominant discourse about poverty, or in challenging it through the overall ethos. Everyone should feel welcome and included when stepping into an Early Years environment. The ethos in a setting comes about through a combination of the physical environment and resources, the way in which the curriculum is experienced alongside the attitudes of the staff who work there. In this way, Apple (2004, p. 5) points out that all educational settings 'act as agents of cultural and ideological hegemony'.

Chapter 2 also described the way in which, since the end of the twentieth century, the burgeoning middle-class experience has been promoted as ever more desirable and, as part of this, the rhetoric around 'escaping' the working class became more powerful and continues to be so. Early Years practitioners and settings play their part in reinforcing these ideas that are conveyed through the environment, the curriculum and much more. In this sense, they play a potentially very influential part in determining the ways in which these hegemonic ideas are first transmitted to young children. This early phase of education is crucial to the way that children learn how to define meaning through understanding what is given value and status in society by way of both the overt and hidden curriculum. As an example, remember that as Hanley (2012) points out, the frequent use of what she calls 'loaded' language, when even an innocuous word like 'estate' has taken on a new and derogatory meaning for some people. Even young children can pick up the nuances of overheard conversations by practitioners that imply that living on an 'estate' is not as desirable as living in other areas. What is provided as part of this early experience of education is important, but equally important is what is *not* experienced. So, for instance, if a child never sees their familiar home environment living in a tower block on an estate being represented in displays, picture books and other resources, how might this make them feel?

Reflecting on all this may conflict with views that Early Years practitioners have previously never needed to challenge. This different approach helps practitioners to become aware of the potential of Early Years Education as a vehicle for social change by 'unveiling a world of oppression and then developing a pedagogy for liberation' (Goodley 2011, p. 154). This is also an approach encouraged by the influential Reggio Emilia approach to Early Years Education first developed in Italy that values the interaction between the child, the teacher and the environment in enabling the 100 languages of children to be heard, listened to and acted upon. It also chimes with the child-centred emphasis that derives from the New Zealand Te Whariki approach and the Mosaic Approach that is built around practitioners listening to children. All these pedagogical influences that place young children as partners in their own learning can be seen in the statutory framework for the Early Years Foundation Stage (DfE 2017).

MacNaughton *et al.* (2007, p. 167) talk about the impact of the concept of a critically self-reflective practitioner who recognises this potential for change, saying that this may depend on the extent to which they perceive their role. They go on to explain that this defines what Gramsci called the split between a 'traditional' intellectual and an 'organic' intellectual undertaking. They interpret Gramsci's view of the intellectual as 'someone who undertakes cultural, social and educational activities that either sustain or challenge particular world views or paradigms.' Those who conform to and reinforce existing interpretations of knowledge are described as 'traditional' intellectuals and thus 'support political and social *stability*', in contrast to 'organic' intellectuals who 'support political and social *change* [italics in original]. These writers suggest that concepts such as rights and diversity are not necessarily recognised or given prominence by the more conformist 'traditional' intellectuals that work in Early Years settings, and that for such ideas to gain leverage in an organisation it is necessary for the 'organic' intellectuals to gain a degree of influence and status. Being able to draw on a range of resources is part of the process of becoming such an 'organic' Early Years practitioner (adapted from Argent 2012).

Campaigning organisations

Individuals may be very knowledgeable about the curriculum, social policy and politics as part of their development as an inclusive practitioner but be unaware of the wealth of information available online from a number of long established campaigning organisations. These can provide valuable links to up-to-date research, local provision of support and can also often offer free resources like information leaflets. In order to develop one's own knowledge and understanding of poverty, an inclusive practitioner has a responsibility to do some additional reading and research. Those organisations that many find particularly helpful in relation to working with children and families living in poverty include the following:

Save the Children was founded in 1919 by the two sisters Eglantyne Jebb and Dorothy Buxton in response to the terrible malnutrition that was rife in cities like Vienna and Berlin as a result of blockades by Britain at the end of World War I. Once the organisation was set up it raised huge amounts of money and brought relief to thousands of children. It continues to campaign and raise money for a wide range of causes throughout the world, including in the UK where their website provides links to a number of evidence-based research reports about the effects of poverty. One of the most recent and shocking *A Fair Start* *for Every Child* was published in 2014. This includes discussion of the impact of poverty on younger children:

> The chances of going without are higher for younger children, who are more likely to be in poverty because their parents stop work temporarily to care for them. They are more likely to be affected by low household income as they spend more time in the home compared with school-aged children; poverty has a greater impact on young children because of the importance of the early years on lifetime development.

It goes on to explain:

> Young children growing up in disadvantaged families are less likely to participate in formal pre-school care, which is designed to provide children with a high-quality early-years learning environment where they can learn skills that will help them in their later school careers. Many families cannot afford to send their children to pre-school because of the cost relative to household income.

There are now several reputable campaigning organisations with the specific remit of providing links to research and other practical information about supporting the various needs of people affected by poverty. These include:

The **Child Poverty Action Group** (CPAG) was established in 1965 by a small group of concerned social workers and sociologists with the specific remit of trying to alleviate the effects of poverty on children by putting pressure on government. It seems that ignorance about the prevalence of poverty was just as problematic at that time as the minutes of their first meeting stated: 'That it would be useful if someone could be appointed who would write the press whenever an occasion arose to bring home to the public the existence of poverty and to correct misapprehensions about the poor'. The organisation is now at the forefront of national campaigning in terms of influencing government policy and also provides training and advice for the people who work with those affected by poverty on subjects like accessing benefits and legal advice.

End Child Poverty is a campaigning movement that was set up in 2003 and is currently hosted by the Child Poverty Action Group. It is composed of over 100 different children's charities, child welfare organisations, social justice groups, faith groups, trade unions and others, with the common aim of working towards the elimination of poverty in the UK. It focuses on gathering evidence about specific concerns in order to put pressure on the government. A recent example is 'Short Changed: The True Cost of Cuts to Children's Benefits' (2016) which concludes that:

> Children have been hardest hit by austerity. This paper shows how significant progress could be made to help them and to reduce child poverty by giving children's benefits the same protection as pensioner benefits. Without this step, families will continue to struggle to make ends meet, pushing more children into poverty.

Shelter provides specific information and advice about housing. It is a campaigning organisation set up in 1966 as a direct response to the public outcry of the television screening of a docu-drama *Cathy Come Home*. This iconic film, which is worth watching if you haven't already seen it, highlighted the terrible living conditions of at least 3 million people living in appalling slum conditions with no legal protection from exploitative landlords. More than 50 years later, this organisation continues to campaign for better affordable housing, fair rents and for the rights of an estimated 100,000 children who have no permanent home.

The Trussell Trust is an example of a foodbank provider. Charitable organisations have become a feature of twenty-first-century family life to provide emergency relief for those who are unable to buy enough food and other necessary household items due to inadequate funds. Many other agencies have become involved in this excellent initiative, including many faith organisations. They work in partnership with professionals who usually refer individuals and families although there are also some self-referrals. They also provide money and debt advice and some offer breakfast and holiday meal clubs. They depend on volunteers to sort the food and other donations and then to dispense these at designated community locations and although thousands of people are currently involved in helping to make them work efficiently, they are always in need of further practical support. It may be that an Early Years setting could be a collection point for donations or practitioners and parents may want to become involved in other ways.

More specific issues are also supported by the work of campaigning organisations, many of which continue to lobby government for changes to improve the experience of people living in difficult situations, including the effects of poverty. For instance, at least 40,000 children in the UK are affected by family imprisonment and this significant life event usually results in a drop in family income, changes to accommodation and many other resulting circumstances that can have a long-term effect on a child's welfare and **i-HOP** is a national one-stop information and advice service to support all professionals in working with children and families of offenders. Finding information from here is relevant to one of the families causing concern for the practitioner Selena in Chapter 6. It may be that the school she works in is unaware of the prevalence of this situation and so Selena could also request further professional development by registering for an online course via i-HOP that supports families of prisoners.

Refugee Action is one of many organisations that provide up-to-date reliable information about the background of asylum seekers, refugees and migrants. It also gives help and advice with regard to individual situations, including struggling with the asylum process, poverty and accessing housing. The website is an excellent source for downloadable resources as well as free leaflets in many community languages. This includes advice for those professionals and Local Authorities working to help individuals to settle in the UK under the government resettlement scheme. As this scheme affects another child in Selena's setting, she may find it useful to find out more about this in order to make the family feel welcome. It may be that professional development for all staff in a setting may be required to understand this complex issue that now affects the lives of well over 65.3 million forcibly displaced people throughout the world (United Nations Refugee Agency 2015).

These are only a fraction of the many organisations that can help practitioners to find out about and understand how to support the needs of individuals and families affected by poverty. There is also a variation of services provided at a local level that needs to be researched.

Picture books

These are the kinds of resources that should be part of every Early Years practitioner's toolkit. There are so many to choose from and all settings will have a wide selection that is made available to children throughout the day. Despite their importance as educational and cultural artefacts, some children do not see many picture books until they experience them outside the home in various educational settings (Whitehead 2010). When they do encounter them, they are usually selected by adults, whether at home or in Early Years settings, to provide an accessible first encounter with the experience of literature. They are often read and re-read with the support of these adults, providing the child with a gateway through which they can make links to their personal experiences and giving them new ways of looking at the world. They require the child to pay close attention to what is conveyed by the pictures and how these are 'explained' by the adult, but also with what lies behind the picture in terms of the subtext – and it is the adult who needs to help develop these complex perceptual and semantic interpretive skills.

Central to these choices are questions about the personal and professional values practitioners operate with and whether, as they progress in their careers, they are encouraged to see picture books as tools that can be used for conveying complex ideas to young children about difference, inequality and social justice and as resources that can be used to challenge negative stereotypes. The initial selection and use of picture books in an Early Years setting conveys powerful messages about what is valued and normal within that setting, and if the range of views and opinions that challenge accepted social norms are not available, then it is likely that children will not develop what the art critic John Berger (1972) calls different 'ways of seeing'. This, of course, has significant implications around the child's developing perception of poverty (adapted from Argent 2016).

So, what does this all mean for Early Years practitioners in terms of how they select picture books to use with young children? I would suggest that the easiest and most enjoyable challenge is to spend some time looking for a wide selection of picture books that represent and reflect the 'ordinary' lives of most of the children in a setting, as building on children's real-life experiences helps to redress an emphasis on what Wrigley (2012, p. 161) describes as the danger of practitioners who are concerned with the effects of poverty focussing on 'moralistic advice on alcohol abuse, unhealthy diets and early pregnancy, underpinned by implicit deficit views of the local area and families'. Picture books can be a powerful way of acknowledging that all children's lives matter. This does not mean that stories about princes and princesses living a life of luxury in castles and children experiencing very materially comfortable lives in huge detached houses should not be included in the mix. The trick is to be aware of the messages that can be conveyed if these are the *only* images that the children see. There are now many excellent contemporary picture books by a range of authors and illustrators, a few of which will now be discussed in further detail.

Through My Window *by Tony Bradman, illustrated by Eileen Browne (Frances Lincoln Ltd)*

I have such fond memories of discovering this book when I was a nursery teacher in inner city Birmingham 30 years ago. Believe it or not, it was then virtually impossible to find any story books that included children from families where one parent was from an ethnic minority. This was extremely frustrating as many of the children at my school were from 'mixed' or what later came to be termed 'dual heritage' backgrounds.

It is a pleasing little story all about Jo, a little girl who lives with her parents in a small maisonette which looks a bit shabby and lived in. But the atmosphere is so cosy and warm using lots of pinks and yellows throughout to help build a homely atmosphere. On the first two pages, we learn that Jo is ill and has to stay at home with her dad looking after her as her mum has to go to work. My goodness, a mother going out

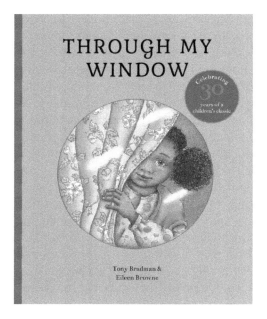

Figure 7.1 *Through My Window* from *Through My Window: Celebrating 30 Years of a Children's Classic* by Tony Bradman and Eileen Browne published by Frances Lincoln Ltd, copyright © 2016. Reproduced by permission of Frances Lincoln Ltd, an imprint of The Quarto Group.

to work – how extraordinary! Actually, it is still very rare to find a picture book where this happens despite it being the experience of many children. As she waves goodbye we get a hint of the busy urban street outside with a Punk strolling across the road and a woman running with a pushchair.

I'm sure we can all remember the guilty pleasure of a day at home being fussed over. As long as one didn't feel too unwell, it was quite a novelty to lie on the sofa with a muddle of toys and books, to eat lunch off a tray etc. You can almost feel the fugginess and stuffiness of the small room contrasted with what looks like a very windy, grey Autumn day outside. The gentle rhythm of the story lies in Jo's anticipation of

So Jo waved goodbye
to her mum
from the window
until she turned the corner
of the street.

Figure 7.2 *Jo Looking out of the Window Illustration* from *Through My Window: Celebrating 30 Years of a Children's Classic* by Tony Bradman and Eileen Browne published by Frances Lincoln Ltd, copyright © 2016. Reproduced by permission of Frances Lincoln Ltd, an imprint of The Quarto Group.

her mother's return with a promised surprise at the end of the day. As she regularly looks out the living room window, she sees all the friendly people living and working in her evidently multicultural community. The next-door neighbour, Mrs Ali, drops in with some comics and stays for a cup of tea. This is an affirmation of peaceful, inner city living, which was (and continues to be) the real-life experience of many children. As the day drags on, boredom sets in but mum is true to her word and when the present is unwrapped at the end of the day it is a doctor's outfit – perfect. The picture of the three of them sitting, tired but contented on the sofa with tired mum's shoes kicked off shouts 'happy family' to me.

Lulu Loves Flowers *by Anna McQuinn,* *illustrated by Rosalind Beardshaw (Alanna Books)*

Figure 7.3 *Lulu Loves Flowers* from *Lulu Loves Flowers* © 2015 Alanna Books, stories by Anna McQuinn, illustrations by Rosalind Beardshaw, published by Alanna Books.

This is the fourth book in the popular and very charming series about Lulu, a 4-year-old little girl who shares plenty of everyday adventures with her readers. The author explains that she is very keen to depict children who come from ordinary backgrounds. Part of this challenges the idea that all children live in houses with gardens so she decided to show her living in an upstairs apartment and so making her garden in an allotment.

Figure 7.4 *Lulu Loves the Library* from *Lulu Loves the Library* © 2006 Alanna Books, stories by Anna McQuinn, illustrations by Rosalind Beardshaw, published by Alanna Books.

Lulu Loves the Library *by Anna McQuinn, illustrated by Rosalind Beardshaw (Alanna Books)*

Lulu loves reading books, which is another strong feature in all of this series, so it is no surprise to see that she makes good use of her local community library to find out helpful gardening information. The availability of free books provided by libraries is an increasingly important message to get across in the climate of cuts to these services.

Another example of reflecting an ordinary background is in the fifth book in the series, *Lulu gets a Cat*, which includes her making a

Figure 7.5 *Lulu Upstairs in Apartment* from *Lulu Loves the Library* © 2006 Alanna Books, stories by Anna McQuinn, illustrations by Rosalind Beardshaw, published by Alanna Books.

Figure 7.6 *Lulu at the Library* from *Lulu Loves the Library* © 2006 Alanna Books, stories by Anna McQuinn, illustrations by Rosalind Beardshaw, published by Alanna Books.

Lulu and Daddy make a special corner where her cat will settle in.

Figure 7.7 *Lulu Making Room Behind the Sofa for Kitty* from *Lulu Gets a Cat* © 2017 Alanna Books, stories by Anna McQuinn, illustrations by Rosalind Beardshaw, published by Alanna Books.

'special place' behind the sofa to help her cat settle into the new house because not all children will live in houses that have a utility room or spare room to do this.

Yolanda Scott, the editorial director of Charlesbridge, which is the US publisher of this series, has written a fascinating and thought-provoking blog that relates to being aware of different circumstances when writing and publishing books for children. Here, she comments on the need to reflect a wide range of backgrounds in children's books, based on her own childhood experiences of living in a family with a limited income:

When my sister and I were kids, we used to play next to (and sometimes on) the dumpsters in the parking lot while my mother cleaned offices. At the age of twenty-two, my mom was a single parent of two small children, putting herself through college while working as a waitress and cleaning lady. We were on food stamps and participated in WIC (Women, Infants and Children) and AFDC (Aid to Families with Dependent Children). I had free lunch at school. Welfare paid for our childcare so my mom could work and take classes and somehow we managed to squeak by.

This made me think about whether I had ever seen any picture books that included young, single parents who are students, juggling their studies with part-time work. I'm not sure that any exist, despite the fact that I myself have taught such students for the last 15 years. Scott goes on to point out the responsibility of editors to apply some guiding principles when they are working on potential books:

- Is it possible that when I edit a text for clarity and brevity, I might be stripping out class markers that the author has included? (Keep in mind that most of my editorial cuts happen well before an illustrator gets to see the text).

- What effect does propagating a middle-class norm have on children either above or below that 'normative' level? How important is it for children to see themselves in a book, and how does that affect their enjoyment of the title?

- Isn't 'middle class' a rather imprecise catch-all anyway? What do I mean by 'poor'? 'Middle class'? 'Rich'?

- How can I better balance the natural impulse to show kids a better (easier/simpler) world with the need to teach them about the one that they live in right now?

- Is it possible to separate class from other labels such as race and gender?

- Can I work harder to understand how my unconscious ideology and the author and illustrator's unconscious ideology are influencing the book?

- Aside from encouraging artists to explore non-suburban settings and on occasion to depict an apartment building instead of a single-family home, what more could I be doing to normalize different socio-economic realities in the books I help shape?

(Scott 2014)

All this happens before a book even reaches publication but it is perhaps helpful for practitioners to apply the same critical questions when they are looking at books to use with children in the setting.

A Visit to City Farm *by Verna Wilkins,*
illustrated by Karin Littlewood (Firetree Books)

As with their earlier picture book *Abdi's Day*, this author and illustrator use a school trip with young children from diverse backgrounds who attend an ordinary urban school as the basis for the plot. This is comfortable and familiar territory for nearly all of us, whether as a childhood memory, as a parent or as an Early Years practitioner. The excitement of the children is palpable as they prepare for the outing to a city farm with their teachers.

The journey is often just as memorable as the final destination and this is an important part of the story. And so, Rainbow class sets off across London walking in a crocodile towards the underground station past the 'howling traffic', along the busy street, stopping to point up at a church steeple and calling out to someone's grandma who works in the flower shop along the way. Once on the train, everyone is helpful and smiley and we get a real sense of the overcrowding, which is balanced on the next double page spread with a sense of space as we look at them arriving at the farm as seen from a distance.

The plot is very straightforward and provides an authentic, cosy and accessible second-hand experience of a visit to a city farm. The soft colourful watercolour illustrations definitely contribute to this atmosphere. Karin Littlewood spent a long time at Chalkhill School in Tower Hamlets drawing real children and this means that she has successfully captured the individuality of expressions and stance with real warmth. I liked the last pages where we see all the animals in the foreground and the children in the distant background, waving goodbye as they leave them behind on the farm.

The publicity for the Australian author and illustrator, Bob Graham explains that he is 'renowned for celebrating the magic of everyday-ness' and he says: 'I'd like reading my books to be a little like opening a family photo album, glimpsing small moments captured from daily lives.' I can only urge you to spend time looking at as many of these as possible because all of them portray such sensitively drawn and realis-tic situations that would chime with the reality of the lives of many chil-dren. He tells universal stories because, although he is Australian, the urban multicultural environments in which these families live have rec-ognisable characteristics, wherever one lives. They are rather scruffy, a bit run down but nevertheless always cosy. I think this is because he focuses on the strong relationships between family members and other people in the community. Nothing bad ever happens in these mean streets, on the contrary they are vibrant busy places where people look out for one another and rub along very well. This is not a romantic view of city life but it is a welcome change from the sometimes-negative por-trayal of such environments in the wider media. It also challenges the more chocolate-box atmosphere of many traditional children's picture books and so presents the reader with a more socially realistic world, where some parents dress in grungy style clothes and have tattoos. The landscapes include high rise flats, the streets have litter in them and shop fronts look a bit battered.

One of my favourites is **Silver Buttons**, with its title beautifully picked out in silver lettering. It initially appealed to me because of the cover where the little girl, wearing glasses is crouched intently over her drawing of a duck in a hat. She holds a silver pen in her hand and is evidently about to add another button to his boots. A baby with his nappy which is precariously slipping down is staggering towards her, and the dog looks up at him, as if he was thinking 'Yikes – I didn't know that you could walk! Please don't wreck the drawing or you will be in so much trouble!'

The first double page spread tells us more about what is going on as we are taken a few minutes back to the time 9.59 on a Thursday morning, before the girl, Jodie, adds the silver buttons and the baby,

Jonathan, is about to push himself to his feet. The dog is sleeping beside them and they are surrounded by the everyday muddle of family life in a restricted living space. Some washing is drying on a clothes rack and there are some toys scattered about, and a child's drawing is pinned on the mantelpiece in pride of place.

On the next pages, we learn that Jonathan's curiosity about the drawing has inspired him to take his first step. We then go into the kitchen and get another intimate glimpse into the life of this family as the young mum sits playing her tin whistle and we see more toys scattered all around and plenty of photos and children's drawings everywhere.

The illustrations take us outside the house into the street and then into the larger town where we see a grandad making a complicated house of leaves with another little girl in the park and an old lady pushing a shopping trolley who 'carried everything she had in two paper bags'. I'm not sure that I have ever seen homelessness depicted so starkly but with such a tender touch in picture books before, despite it being all around us in reality.

This is a powerful story about family and community that conveys the importance of treasuring little moments and letting children know every day that they are valued and loved. It is no surprise to see that it is endorsed by Amnesty International, an organisation that states 'Every one of us has the right to experience justice, fairness, freedom and truth in our lives. These important values are our human rights'.

Another one by Bob Graham is **Oscar's Half Birthday**, which begins with a picture of a young family living in a flat. Dad is leaning over the breakfast counter and mum sits with the two children and dog on the sofa in a clutter of toys and books. They decide to go on a journey to the park to celebrate the baby Oscar's 'half birthday'. First, they have to wait for the lift to arrive and the little girl stands on tip toe to press the buttons as they wait patiently with the pushchair surrounded by graffiti-covered walls. Then they walk together through the busy streets until they arrive at the park where it seems as if 'the whole town is up here'. After all the excitement, they return to the flat and the two children enjoy a bath together with lots more friendly clutter all around them, and later on mum and dad dance together in the living room area, having first taken up the rug and moved aside some furniture. Once again, this book gives a strong message about a happy family living in very ordinary, modest circumstances.

Where to find books like these?

Several years ago, I did some research with nursery school practitioners about where they looked for the picture books to be used in their settings. It emerged that most people relied on recommendations by the library but Chapter 6 includes some discussion about the declining role of libraries due to local funding cutbacks, so this may no longer be an easy option. Other reasons for buying particular books were recommendations by commercial book providers that usually offered an attractive discount as an incentive for bulk buying. Sometimes choices about buying books would also be influenced by a particular professional interest or by children in their own families (Argent 2016). Other available recommendations can be found via reputable websites including BookTrust, The Literacy Trust, Letterbox Library and The Letterpress Project, which all provide reviews and information about books for young children. As well as doing online research, browse the wonderful selection available in local bookshops as handling a book and spending time looking closely at the pictures is time very well spent. Make a note of all those that impress you and then talk knowledgeably about these with others in your workplace who may have responsibility for buying new books. It is also worth looking regularly at the book selection in local charity shops as those in good condition can be bought at relatively low prices.

Apart from providing a wide range of books to be used and enjoyed by the children as part of the curriculum provision, a small lending library is a wonderful community resource in any Early Years setting and can also include a range of story sacks that include a book inside plus toys and props to enable children and their parents to retell stories through their play. So, for example, *Goldilocks and the Three Bears* would have three bears, bowls, spoons, chairs and beds of various sizes plus a girl doll. These were first invented by Neil Griffiths, now a successful educational consultant who, when he was a head teacher, encouraged parents in his school to help make these resources. Commercial versions are now available but staff and parents all over the world now also make their own, much cheaper bespoke story sacks (Argent 2016).

This is the kind of practical community project that can be really exciting and inclusive in any Early Years setting as parents and other family members from all kinds of backgrounds can come together regularly, perhaps using the staff room as a base to share stories and make story sacks together with materials provided.

Toy libraries

There may be an assumption that most children have plenty of toys and activities to play with in their homes, whereas this is not the case. Save the Children (2014) points out that 'Many children from poorer families will also lack the toys and access to activities, both within and outside of the home, that stimulate their development'. Those living in temporary accommodation will be living in communal, shared spaces where personal property of all kinds may be difficult to look after. A transient lifestyle also means that items like toys can get mislaid or lost in the muddle of everything else. Many children live in housing that is overcrowded, which may mean little space for many toys and a garden is not something that everyone has easy access to. Libraries, children's centres, charities and many nurseries used to offer the loan of toys alongside books as a way of ensuring that all children could access and enjoy good quality resources whatever their circumstances. The rationale was that many families struggled to provide a range of toys appropriate to different ages and stages and also that many homes had limited storage facilities. Toy libraries were organised in much the same way as traditional libraries and parents were able to borrow a number of items to take home on a regular basis, sometimes the toy library would only be open one day per week but this soon became part of a routine and was much appreciated. Staffing such a wonderful resource requires considerable organisation and co-ordination as well as facilities for storage and by phoning around a number of children's centres in different parts of the country, it seems that toy libraries are now rarely included as a service to local families:

> A much-loved toy library is to close at the end of the month after finally admitting defeat in its battle to continue amid the tough economic climate. The announcement will come as heart breaking news to the 200 or so families whose children regularly visit the Borrower's Toy Library, in Barnards Green, to pick and choose from its range of more than 10,000 toys.
>
> (*Malvern Gazette Online* 9 March 2012)

Practitioners explained that they require appropriate storage, high levels of maintenance, administration and ongoing promotion that no longer fit with the priorities of a severely reduced service. Many authorities now prioritise outreach services due to reorganisation as a result of cuts to funding rather than those located in a centre and so this would present other problems. However, it may be that an individual school or nursery might consider offering this community service because toys in very good condition can be easily sourced from charity shops, car boot sales, bazaars and jumble sales and donations of used toys can be requested.

Conclusion

This chapter has explained how Early Years practitioners can access a wealth of information about campaigning organisations in order to improve their own knowledge and understanding about poverty and how this affects many families. These organisations can also provide valuable advice and support with respect to issues like debt management, benefits and housing. The use of picture books that reflect a wide range of backgrounds contributes to an inclusive learning environment for all children. I have suggested a few examples from my own professional experience that I believe would be excellent additions to any Early Years book collection. Finding others requires Early Years practitioners to be aware of the range that is available, know where to find such titles and to think carefully about how such positive representations of ordinary lives can have a significant effect on how individual children and their families feel valued.

The revised Early Years Foundation Stage (EYFS) (2017) supports the importance of providing an inclusive learning environment that meets the needs of all children. This is significant in terms of the knowledge, understanding and attitudes of all staff working in the setting, strong respectful partnerships with all families and the resources that are made available. The provision of toy libraries and story sacks in an Early Years setting are just two examples of how access to a range of imaginative experiences that would be beneficial for all children could be provided.

References

Al Rasheed, T. (2012) 'Toy Library is to Close due to Lack of Funding', in *Malvern Gazette online*, 9 March 2012. Available online at: www.malverngazette.co.uk/news/9580440.Toy_library_is_to_close_due_to_lack_of_funding/ (accessed: 6 May 2017).

Amnesty International. Available online at: www.amnesty.org.uk/ (accessed: 15 May 2017).

Apple, M.W. (2004) *Ideology and Curriculum*, 3rd edition. London: Routledge-Falmer.

Argent, K. (2012) 'Understanding Disability in Nursery Schools', postgraduate thesis. Available online at: www.letterpressproject.co.uk/the-resource-archive/2016-04-15/powerful-picture-books-understanding-disability-in-nursery-schools (accessed: 4 May 2017).

Argent, K. (2016) 'Caught or Taught – Developing a Love of Reading: Neil Griffiths'. Available online at: www.letterpressproject.co.uk/inspiring-young-readers/2016-07-19/caught-or-taught-developing-a-love-of-reading-neil-griffiths (accessed: 4 May 2017).

Bradman, T. and Browne, E. (2016) *Through My Window: Celebrating 30 Years of a Children's Classic*. London: Frances Lincoln Ltd.

CPAG (n. d.) 'Minutes of first meeting CPAG meeting in 1965'. Available online at: http://www.cpag.org.uk/content/minutes-first-cpag-meeting-0 (accessed: 4 May 2017).

Department for Education (2017) *Statutory Framework for the Early Years Foundation Stage*. Available online at: www.foundationyears.org.uk/files/2017/03/EYFS_STATUTORY_FRAMEWORK_2017.pdf (accessed: 15 May 2017).

End Child Poverty (2016) 'Short Changed: The True Cost of Cuts to Children's Benefits' Available online at: www.endchildpoverty.org.uk/wpcontent/uploads/2015/07/PDF_Short_Changed_fullreport.pdf (accessed: 4 May 2017).

Goodley, D. (2011) *Disability Studies*. London: Sage Publications Ltd.

Graham, B. (2008) *Oscar's Half Birthday*. London: Walker Books.

Graham, B. (2013) *Silver Buttons*. London: Walker Books.

Hanley, L. (2012) *Estates*. London: Granta.

i-HOP. Available online at: www.i-hop.org.uk/app/about_us. (accessed: 4 May 2017).

MacNaughton, G., Hughes, P. & Smith, K. (2007) 'Early childhood professionals and children's rights: tensions and possibilities around the United Nations General Comment No. 7 on Children's Rights', *International Journal of Early Years Education*, 15, (2), pp. 161–170.

McQuinn, A. (2015) *Lulu Loves Flowers*. London: Alanna Books.

McQuinn, A. (2017) *Lulu gets a Cat*. London: Alanna Books.

Refugee Action (n. d.) Available online at: www.refugee-action.org.uk/ (accessed: 4 May 2017).

Save The Children (2014) *A Fair Start for Every Child*. Available online at: www.savethechildren.org.uk/sites/default/files/images/A_Fair_Start_for_Every_Child.pdf (accessed: 4 May 2017).

Scott, Y. (2014) 'Dumpster Diving: An Observation on Class in Children's Books'. Available online at: www.cbcdiversity.com/post/68979098613/dumpster-diving-an-observation-on-class-in (accessed: 4 May 2017).

Shelter. Available online at: http://england.shelter.org.uk/ (accessed: 4 May 2017).

The Trussell Trust. Available online at: https://www.trusselltrust.org/ (accessed: 4 May 2017).

UNHCR 'Figures at a Glance'. Available online at: www.unhcr.org/uk/figures-at-a-glance.html (accessed: 4 May 2017).

Whitehead, M. (2010) *Language and Literacy in the Early Years 0-7*, 4th edition. London: Sage Publications Ltd.

Wilkins, V. (2016) *A Visit to City Farm*. Firetree Books: London.

Wrigley, T. 'Rethinking Poverty and Social Class: The Teacher's Response' in R. Arshad, T. Wrigley and L. Pratt (eds.) (2012) *Social Justice re-examined*. London: Institute of Education Press.

8 Conclusion

Chris Collett

This book has discussed the social construction of poverty, within the current policy context, and interrogated some of the common discourses that attempt to explain this growing phenomenon and seek for solutions. The book argues that there is a simplified approach to understanding poverty, which focuses on blaming individuals whilst disregarding wider and more complex structural explanations. It examines the role of Early Years Education in challenging these misconceptions and aims to equip Early Years practitioners to identify the disadvantages faced by children and families living in poverty, and offer effective and non-judgemental support.

The UK is in the top ten wealthiest countries in the world and yet since the late 1990s the number of children living in poverty has grown exponentially, and is increasing; one in four children is currently growing up in poverty (CPAG 2017). Between 1 April 2016 and 31 March 2017, The Trussell Trust's Foodbank Network provided 1,182,954 emergency food supplies to people in crisis compared to 1,109,309 in 2015–16. Of this number, 436,938 went to children. This is a measure of volume rather than unique users, and on average, people needed two foodbank referrals in the last year (Trussell 2017). In recent years, so-called 'benefit reform', alongside cuts to support services have exacerbated what was already a growing issue.

The impact of poverty on young children is profound and long lasting, affecting all aspects of development, and children from poorer backgrounds lag behind their more affluent peers, at all stages of education. Children born in the poor areas of the UK have on average a lower birthweight, are more likely to die at birth or in infancy and are more likely to have a disability or to suffer chronic illness during childhood than children born into richer families. They are almost twice as likely to live in poor housing, which further significantly affects physical and mental health, as well as educational achievement. And there are tangible social consequences. Children from poor families can miss school (for lack of suitable clothing) and school trips; can't invite friends round for tea; and can't afford a one-week holiday away from home (CPAG 2017).

Although overwhelming evidence points to the effects of institutional disadvantage on poverty and social exclusion, the dominant discourse focuses on individual behavioural explanations that cite poor life choices and has hardened public attitudes, especially towards the working-class poor, characterising and 'othering' them as a distinct homogenous group with particular features, and often labelling them with negative terminology. There has been a return to the nineteenth-century notion of the 'deserving' and 'undeserving' poor, with an emphasis on the latter, with the idea that many of those living in poverty – particularly where there is intergenerational poverty – choose that way of life and so 'only have themselves to blame'. Fuelled by the media, representations of the poor working class paint a picture of a whole sector of the population who are lazy and feckless, leeching off society through benefit dependency. Stories of benefit fraud are seized upon, whilst the reality of the tax evasion and avoidance practices of the rich are conveniently overlooked, or receive only minimum coverage.

Any debate around structural causes of poverty, such as social class, has become unfashionable, giving way instead to ideas about 'meritocracy' in which all have the opportunity to do well. However, this explanation fails to take into account the hidden advantages of the middle class and the institutional discrimination to which the poor working class are often subjected. Despite its relative affluence, wealth inequality in the UK is high, and the ever-widening gap between the richest and poorest brings with it a host of social issues, including high rates of crime and mental ill health, with correspondingly low levels of social mobility, meaning that children who are born poor are likely to remain poor.

But poverty is not simply about denial of material wealth. Bourdieu recognised the wider resources that are necessary for success; namely social and cultural capital, something which children of well-off, educated middle-class parents have in abundance. Since these dominant middle-class values also underpin the design and implementation of our education system, it is little wonder that their counterparts from poorer, working class backgrounds who may not have access to the social networks, cultural experiences and sophisticated language styles associated with these types of capital, begin their educational life at a significant disadvantage.

In this context, more than ever, it is the responsibility of individual Early Years practitioners to be aware of the extent to which their understanding of poverty may be influenced by biased messages from government and the media that almost exclusively buy into behavioural explanations for poverty, but that are founded on sparse evidence. Practitioners need to think creatively about how meaningful relationships with families can be built and maintained, taking an expansive approach to what might constitute children's families and resisting the deficit and compensatory model associated with incendiary labels of 'good' and 'bad' parents. Practitioners can make a difference, ensuring that the ethos of the setting makes it clear that all children and their families are welcome, via a combination of positive and non-judgemental staff attitudes and resources within the physical environment. To ensure this, practitioners need to have some knowledge of relevant campaigning organisations and what they can offer in terms of research evidence plus support and advice, and consider the practicalities of making information available to colleagues and families on issues like debt management and housing, without stigmatising.

The EYFS curriculum places an emphasis on the importance of an inclusive environment for all children. A key factor in fostering a sense of belonging for all children is the availability of a good range of picture books that reflect the spectrum of family situations experienced by children. These positive representations of ordinary lives can have a significant effect on how individual children and their families feel valued, and can be both informative and encourage discussion and reflection.

It's important also, for practitioners to be aware of how many families will have limited space at home and limited incomes, which may mean lack of access to a variety of toys and activities outside the setting, particularly in school holidays. These can be supplemented in practical ways, by the setting making available resources such as story sacks and a toy library.

Approaches to working in partnership are naturally influenced by practitioners' personal and professional experiences, but it is important that practitioners avoid judging parents on their behaviour and choices. Instead negative stereotypes and attitudes towards children who may be experiencing the effects of poverty should be challenged, and support offered to children and families who may be in this position.

Wrigley (2012) notes that the relationships between professionals and 'poor' parents are often characterised by a kind of 'preachiness', which has been given licence by the increasing trend in governments who are prone to lecture the populace about healthy lifestyles. I've often heard practitioners criticising parents who they know to be receiving help, for choosing to spend money on, for example, a new television, or because perhaps one or other parent smokes. From the practitioner's perspective, these might not seem like the 'correct' priorities in a family where money is short. But the implication here is that poor parents cannot (and therefore should not) be trusted to make their own choices. It should be remembered that in our democracy, alongside an entitlement to a certain standard of living and quality of life, it is a basic human right to enjoy freedom of choice and self-determination. We have to consider how we ourselves would feel, if choice and agency were removed. Therefore, it falls to practitioners to respect the decisions that *all* parents make, even when they do not coincide with our own.

The importance of working in partnership with parents in Early Years settings has long been taken as read, and remains central to the EYFS (2017), placing the onus on Early Years practitioners to find effective ways of facilitating this. Partnership working with parents and agencies from different sectors has had many different manifestations, and the quality of these professional interactions can vary widely across settings. But there are many good practice examples, such as Solihull, as described in Chapter 6, and from which we can see that when applied well, the principles of Early Support can be positive and effective. Creating respectful partnerships, early intervention and prevention are as important as managing risks and reducing harm and will have long-term benefits for everyone. Practitioners need to do some research to learn more about what is available and how agencies relate to one another. An inclusive school community is a caring one that knows where and when to offer support and to signpost to specialist services. But working in partnership is not without its challenges, which have been compounded by the current cuts to services.

Killeen (2008) argues that both poverty and discrimination against the poor run contrary to the spirit and the terms of the Universal Declaration on Human Rights and the human rights framework could provide a mechanism for change. Poverty is not a protected characteristic of equalities legislation, so there is no protection against discrimination and prejudice. But the acknowledgement of human rights presents a challenge to current government ideology and, if anything, an already significant erosion of rights legislation looks likely to continue. We are living through changing times and whatever the next government chooses to do with respect to poverty, Early Years practitioners have to take responsibility for ensuring that they work within and beyond the constraints, to ensure that the rights of children and families are honoured.

References

Child Poverty Action Group (2017) Available online at www.cpag.org.uk/content/impact-poverty (accessed: May 2017).

EYFS (2017) Available online at www.foundationyears.org.uk/files/2017/03/EYFS_STATUTORY_FRAMEWORK_2017.pdf (accessed: May 2017).

Killeen, D. (2008) *Is Poverty in the UK a Denial of People's Human Rights?* York: Joseph Rowntree Foundation Publications.

Trussell Trust (2017) Available online at https://www.trusselltrust.org/2017/04/25/uk-foodbank-use-continues-rise/ (accessed: May 2017).

Index